Revolutions: A Very Short Introduction

VERY SHORT INTRODUCTIONS are for anyone wanting a stimulating and accessible way in to a new subject. They are written by experts and have been translated into more than 40 different languages. The series began in 1995 and now covers a wide variety of topics in every discipline. The VSI library contains nearly 400 volumes—a Very Short Introduction to everything from Indian philosophy to psychology and American history--and continues to grow in every subject area.

Very Short Introductions available now:

For more information visit our web site

www.oup.co.uk/general/vsi/

Jack A. Goldstone

REVOLUTIONS

A Very Short Introduction

OXFORD
UNIVERSITY PRESS

OXFORD
UNIVERSITY PRESS

Oxford University Press is a department of the University of Oxford.
It furthers the University's objective of excellence in research,
scholarship, and education by publishing worldwide.

Oxford   New York
Auckland   Cape Town   Dar es Salaam   Hong Kong   Karachi
Kuala Lumpur   Madrid   Melbourne   Mexico City   Nairobi
New Delhi   Shanghai   Taipei   Toronto

With offices in
Argentina   Austria   Brazil   Chile   Czech Republic   France   Greece
Guatemala   Hungary   Italy   Japan   Poland   Portugal   Singapore
South Korea   Switzerland   Thailand   Turkey   Ukraine   Vietnam

Oxford is a registered trademark of Oxford University Press
in the UK and certain other countries.

Published in the United States of America by
Oxford University Press
198 Madison Avenue, New York, NY 10016

Library of Congress Cataloging-in-Publication Data
Goldstone, Jack A.
Revolutions : a very short introduction / Jack A. Goldstone.
pages   cm.—(Very short introductions)
Includes bibliographical references and index.
ISBN 978-0-19-985850-7 (pbk.)
1. Revolutions—History. I. Title.
D21.3.G65   2014
303.6'409—dc23   2013035444

1 3 5 7 9 8 6 4 2

Printed in Great Britain
by Ashford Colour Press Ltd., Gosport, Hants.
on acid-free paper

To my wife, Gina, who makes everything possible

Contents

List of illustrations

Acknowledgments

I am grateful to fellow scholars of revolution for their comments on parts of the manuscript:

Mark Beissinger, Steven Cook, William Doyle, John Foran, Stephen Haber, Richard Hamilton, Mark Kishlansky, Alan Knight, Charles Kurzman, John Markoff, Ian Morris, Sharon Erickson Nepstad, John Padgett, Silvia Pedraza, Elizabeth Perry, Eric Selbin, S. A. Smith, Walter Scheidel, and Gordon Wood. They have saved me from many errors; I bear responsibility for those that remain.

I also owe major debts to my editors at Oxford University Press—Nancy Toff, Joellyn Ausanka, and Max Richman—for their encouragement, support, exacting review, and superb execution of this volume. Their insistence on quality in every respect is a model for editors.

My wonderful wife, Gina Saleman-Goldstone, reviewed each chapter for clarity and style; if this book is easy and enjoyable to read, the credit goes to her.

ACKNOWLEDGMENTS

I am grateful to a few scholars...

Chapter 1
What is a revolution?

On the morning of July 14, 1789, a crowd of Parisian workers set out to attack the royal prison of the Bastille. Joined by deserting soldiers who brought cannons, and ignored by Royal Army troops camped nearby, the crowds forced their way into the fortress by late afternoon, killing the governor and parading his head on a pike. That evening King Louis XVI reportedly asked the Duc de la Rochefoucauld, "Is this a revolt?" To which the duc replied: "No Sire, it is a *revolution*!"

The duc's answer was shaped by his awareness that the crowds of Paris were not simply demanding lower prices for bread, or the dismissal of an unpopular minister, or protesting the selfish luxury of the queen, Marie Antoinette. They were acting in support of the National Assembly, led by the representatives of the Third Estate, or commoners, to the Estates General. Three weeks earlier, the assembly had defied the king and declared that they, not the Estates of the Nobles or the Clergy, were the true leaders of France. If they were supported by the people and the military defected to join them, the old social and political order of France would be over.

Two great visions shape our views of revolution. One is the heroic vision of revolution. In this view, downtrodden masses are raised up by leaders who guide them in overthrowing unjust rulers, enabling the people to gain their freedom and dignity. Though revolutions are violent, this is necessary to destroy the old regime and vanquish its supporters—the birth pangs of a new order that will provide social justice. This ideal, rooted in Greek and Roman traditions of the founding of republics, was promoted by defenders of the American and French Revolutions such as Thomas Paine and Jules Michelet. It was later given modern form as a theory of the inevitable triumph of the poor over the rich by Karl Marx, Vladimir Lenin, Mao Zedong, and their followers.

Yet there is a second, opposing vision, that revolutions are eruptions of popular anger that produce chaos. In this view, however well meaning, reformers who unleash the mob find the masses demanding blood and creating waves of violence that destroy even the revolutionary leaders. Chasing unrealistic visions and their own glory, revolutionary leaders lay waste to civilized society and bring unwarranted death and destruction. This view was promoted by English critics who feared the excesses of the French Revolution, from Edmund Burke and Thomas Carlyle to Charles Dickens. It was later taken up by critics of the Russian and Chinese revolutions who emphasized the human costs of the transformations pursued by Stalin and Mao.

In reality, the history of revolution reveals both faces. Actual revolutions are enormously varied. Some are nonviolent whereas others produce bloody civil wars; some have produced democracies and greater liberty whereas others have produced brutal dictatorships. Today, political leaders are less concerned with the contending myths of revolution than with understanding why revolutions occur and how they evolve. Revolutions erupting in unexpected places—in Iran and Nicaragua in 1979, in the Soviet Union and Eastern Europe in 1989–91, and across the Arab world in 2011—have not only come as shocks to rulers but have unsettled the international order.

This book seeks to answer the questions of why revolutions occur and why they surprise us, how they have developed over the course of history, and where they have shaped national and global politics. But first we need to have a clear idea of precisely what a revolution is, and how revolutions differ from other kinds of disorders and social change.

Defining "revolution"

Throughout history, people have suffered from misfortune and oppression. Most of the time, people respond with fortitude and resignation, or prayer and hope. Those who suffer usually see the forces in power as too great to change and view themselves as too isolated and weak to be agents of change. Even when people do rebel against authorities, most such acts remain isolated and are easily put down.

Revolutions are thus rare—much rarer than the instances of oppression and injustice. They arise only when rulers become weak and isolated, when elites begin to attack the government rather than defend it, and when people believe themselves to be part of a numerous, united, and righteous group that can act together to create change.

Scholars of politics and history have defined revolution in different ways. Most agree that revolutions involve a forcible change in government, mass participation, and a change in institutions. But some have argued that revolutions must be relatively sudden; others that they entail violence. Some insist that revolutions involve class-based struggles of the poor against the rich, or the common against the privileged. Yet in fact revolutions are diverse in these respects.

In the Chinese Communist Revolution, Mao Zedong spent more than twenty years in the countryside mobilizing the peasantry and fighting the Nationalist regime before taking power. Most of the recent "color" revolutions, such as the People Power Revolution in the Philippines and the Orange Revolution in the Ukraine, were rapid, unfolding in weeks; yet they remained nonviolent. And many anticolonial revolutions—such as the American Revolution—pitted members of all classes against the colonial power, and produced little or no redistribution of wealth or social status.

For much of the twentieth century, social scientists were reluctant to deal with the subjective side of revolution. These "structuralists" preferred to focus on the more easily observed features of conflict and institutional change. Yet in recent years, students of revolution have come to realize how critical the ideologies and narratives of social justice are to revolutionary mobilization and revolutionary outcomes. The pursuit of social justice is inseparable from how people define their revolutionary identities and frame their actions.

We can therefore best define revolution in terms of *both* observed mass mobilization and institutional change, *and* a driving ideology carrying a vision of social justice. *Revolution* is the forcible overthrow of a government through mass mobilization (whether military or civilian or both) in the name of social justice, to create new political institutions.

What revolutions are not

A key difficulty in defining revolutions is separating them from similar, more common disruptive events, particularly since such events almost always occur as part of revolutions. These component events include peasant revolts, grain riots, strikes, social and reform movements, coup d'états, and civil wars. All of these have their own causes and outcomes, but only under certain conditions do they lead to revolutions.

Peasant revolts are uprisings of rural villages. They sometimes aim at resisting the demands of local landlords, sometimes at foiling state agents (tax collectors or other officials). Usually they seek to call attention to exceptional local hardships. Most often, their goal is to get help from the government to resolve local problems, not to change the government itself.

Grain riots are mass mobilizations to protest food shortages or excessively high prices. They involve seizures of grain shipments or stores, attacks on bakeries or merchants, and—in the style of Robin Hood—efforts to distribute food to the poor, and demands to enforce a maximum price or secure state subsidies. They usually occur in cities, where people depend on buying grain and other necessities at market prices, but they can also occur in rural areas at key points for the transit or storage of grain. Grain riots arose in more than a dozen African countries in the wake of high global food prices in 2007–8. Like peasant revolts, they usually seek government help rather than to change the government.

Strikes are mobilizations of workers to withhold work from employers. They usually focus on workplace issues of pay, hours, safety, and work rules, and are local to a particular region or industry. However, if workers have widely shared grievances against government policies they may seek a general strike, in which workers throughout the country refuse to work, or a political strike, in which workers in key industries (mining, energy, transport) coordinate a refusal to work until the government policies in question are changed. Such strikes were crucial in bringing down the Soviet and other communist regimes in Eastern Europe.

Peasant revolts and grain riots are typical of traditional agricultural societies. In most modern societies, by contrast, protests against government policies take the form of social or reform movements. Social movements are mass mobilizations on behalf of particular groups or causes. They commonly focus on discrimination or oppression against members of the group. Social movements can be disruptive and provoke regime violence, as with the civil rights and anti-Vietnam war movements in the United

5

States. They employ such tactics as sit-ins, marches, boycotts, and occupations of state buildings or public places. Nonetheless, most social movements simply aim to resolve the grievances of a particular group.

Reform movements explicitly seek to change existing government institutions. They may seek new laws to limit corruption, or voting rights for more people, or greater autonomy for a region. Yet rather than seeking to overthrow the existing government, they try to attain their goals by working through lawful procedures for institutional change, seeking to win court rulings or electoral campaigns, pass new laws, or obtain constitutional changes. They become revolutionary only when the government resists or delays meaningful change and lashes out at reformers. Thus the Mexican Revolution was unleashed when the dictator Porfirio Díaz jailed the moderate reformer Francisco Madero and manipulated the results of elections that reformers appear to have won.

These sorts of disorders and movements usually aim at remedying local or group grievances. Other kinds of events, however, do aim to overthrow the government. These include coups, radical social movements, and civil wars. But these do not usually produce revolutions either.

The most common acts that result in the forcible overthrow of governments are elite coups or coups d'état (literally, blows to the state). They occur when one authoritarian leader or a small group of leaders takes over the government, without any large mass mobilization or civil struggle. Although military coups against democracies or monarchies produce new political institutions, they hardly ever do so in the name of broad principles of social justice. Rather, the coup leaders usually claim their actions were necessary to restore order, end intolerable corruption, or halt economic decay, and that they will step down once their task is done. Recent military coups in Thailand in 2006 and in Niger in 2010 are good examples.

On the other hand, coups can lead to revolutions if the coup leaders or their followers present a vision for reshaping society on new principles of justice and social order, embark on a program of mass mobilization to build support for that vision, and then enact that vision by creating new institutions. Attaturk's secular nationalist revolution in Turkey, Nasser's Arab nationalist revolution in Egypt, and the Portuguese Officers' Revolution are all cases in point.

Radical social movements, unlike most social movements, seek to forcibly overthrow the state. Yet these do not become effective revolutionary movements unless they move beyond their usually small circle of followers to create a broad coalition of varied groups that share this goal. Otherwise—like the poor student rebels in Victor Hugo's *Les Misérables*—they are easily isolated and suppressed.

Civil wars often produce the forcible overthrow of governments. They can arise from dynastic contests that pit claimants from the same family tree against each other; from military officers falling out and competing for power using their armed supporters; or from religious or ethnic groups seeking to oust or expel their rivals. But in none of these cases is the effort to overthrow the government driven by the dream of realizing a new vision of social justice. Only when a leader with a revolutionary vision builds an army to overthrow the government in order to realize that vision do we speak of a revolutionary war—and if that campaign succeeds and then transforms political institutions, then it is a revolution.

Revolutionary civil wars also arise after the old regime has already been overthrown. Those who enjoyed privileges under the old regime, or even those simply resisting unwelcome changes, may mobilize counterrevolutionary forces and go to war against the new revolutionary government. Some of the most massive civil wars in history, such as the Russian Whites against the Red Army in 1918–21, and the Mexican Civil War of 1913–20, both of which killed millions, arose when revolutionary leaders struggled against counterrevolutions.

In addition to the aforementioned events, one often hears the terms "rebellions, uprisings, insurrections, and guerrilla wars" used when talking about revolutions. These are general terms that are sometimes conflated with "revolution" but do not mean the same thing. A rebellion is any act by a group or individual that refuses to recognize, or seeks to overturn, the authority of the existing government. Thus one can have an elite rebellion, as when courts refuse to recognize a decree of the ruler; or one can have a popular rebellion, as when crowds occupy a public square and refuse to obey government demands that they disperse.

Any attempt at revolution is by definition a rebellion, so efforts to overthrow a regime but fail are often called rebellions. Still, not every rebellion that succeeds leads to revolution. If a duke with dynastic claims to the throne takes up arms against the king, that is a rebellion. But if the duke succeeds and becomes the new king, and all the institutions of government remain much the same, then no revolution has occurred. Uprisings and insurrections are types of popular rebellions—uprisings are usually unarmed or primitively armed popular rebellions, while insurrections involve some degree of military training and organization, and the use of military weapons and tactics by the rebels.

Guerrilla warfare is simply a style of warfare often used in rebellions and revolutions. Whereas conventional warfare relies on fighters who are massed in large-scale military units in regular formations, and who are housed in barracks and supplied by military supply trains, guerrilla warfare relies on smaller numbers of mobile fighters, in irregular-sized units, living off the land or blending into and supplied by the local population. Guerrilla warfare is particularly useful for small forces trying to expel a larger, more powerful force from their territory by inflicting a steady stream of losses while avoiding pitched battles with the more powerful foe. It is therefore often chosen by revolutionaries who are initially few in number and facing a powerful government. The Chinese Communists, the Viet Cong, Castro's forces in Cuba, and the Nicaraguan Sandinistas all used guerrilla warfare. However, as the numbers of their supporters increased and they gained access to more resources (often from abroad), they shifted to more conventional warfare in the final struggle for power.

Peasant revolts, grain riots, strikes, social movements, coups, and civil wars thus all can arise in the course of revolutions and are important constituent elements of revolutionary struggles. Nevertheless, a revolution is something distinct from any of these alone. What gives revolutions their distinctive role in history and in the popular imagination is that only revolutions combine *all* the elements of forcible overthrow of the government, mass mobilization, the pursuit of a vision of social justice, and the creation of new political institutions. It is this combination that leads us to conceive of revolutions as the process by which visionary leaders draw on the power of the masses to forcibly bring into existence a new political order.

Chapter 2
What causes revolutions?

A common misperception about revolutions is that they are acts of frustration—they happen when people say "We're mad as hell and we won't take it anymore." Yet scholarly research has shown that this view is wrong.

Let us start by asking—"won't take any more of *what?*" One possible answer is poverty: when people are so poor that their very survival is threatened, they rebel. This is not entirely wrong, for economic grievances often play a role in rebellions. Yet poverty is generally *not* associated with revolution. The worst poverty usually arises in the wake of crop failures and famines, yet the majority of famines—such as the great Irish potato famine of the 1840s—did not lead to revolutions.

In fact, revolutions occur more often in middle-income countries than in the very poorest nations. When the American Revolution occurred, the American colonists were far better off than European peasants. Even in Europe, the French Revolution of 1789 arose in a country whose peasants were generally better off than the peasants of Russia, where revolution did not occur until more than a hundred years later.

This is because poor peasants and workers cannot overthrow the government when faced with professional military forces determined to defend the regime. Revolutions can occur only when significant portions of the elites, and especially the military, defect or stand aside. Indeed, in most revolutions it is the elites who mobilize the population to help them overthrow the regime.

Some scholars, recognizing that sheer poverty may produce popular revolts but not revolutions, have argued that it is *relative* deprivation that drives revolution—when inequality or class differences grow unbearable, or when people's expectations for further progress are dashed, they rise up in protest. But extreme inequality can just as easily lead to resignation and despair as to revolution; deep inequality also leaves the poor without the resources to create an effective revolutionary force. Throughout most of human history, great inequality and severe poverty have been justified by religion and tradition as natural and inevitable, and have been tolerated, even accepted, as the normal order of things.

What turns poverty or inequality into a motivation for revolution? It is the belief that these conditions are not inevitable but arise from the faults of the regime. Only when elites and popular groups blame the regime for unjust conditions—whether arising from the regime's incompetence, corruption, or favoritism for certain groups at the expense of others—will people rise against it.

Yet another force blamed for revolutions is modernization. In the 1960s and 1970s, when revolutions were breaking out across the developing world, this view had great appeal. Many observers argued that as preindustrial societies start to modernize, people encounter free markets for goods and services, inequality rises, and traditional religious and customary patterns of authority lose their power. As traditional relationships break down, people demand new, more responsive political regimes and turn to force to create them.

With more study, however, it became clear that modernization was not a single package of changes that arrived everywhere in the same way. In some countries modernizing changes undermined regimes and gave rise to revolutions; but in other countries modernizing changes strengthened rulers and created more powerful authoritarian regimes (Saudi Arabia today or Germany under Bismarck). In still others, such as Canada, modernization brought a relatively smooth transition to democracy. In a few nations revolutions occurred just as modernization was beginning, as in Japan in 1868 and China in 1911. Yet in other nations revolutions occurred long after modernization had been largely accomplished, as in Eastern Europe in 1989–91. Clearly, modernization has no consistent relationship to the onset of revolutions.

Finally, some observers attribute revolutions to the spread of new ideologies. This view too has some truth, as ideological shifts play an important role in revolutionary mobilization. Yet this does not explain why people would be drawn to dangerous new political ideas. Rulers and elites usually enforce beliefs that justify their rule, while harshly punishing those who question their authority. So revolutionary ideologies often languish without followers. New ideologies produce revolutionary actions only when there has already been a shift in elite positions, which creates space and opportunities to mobilize people around new beliefs. New ideologies are a part of the story of revolutions. But their appearance is not sufficient to produce revolutionary change.

The reason that all these views of revolutionary causation are inadequate is that they treat society as a passive structure—like a concrete wall—that will crumble when sufficient force is applied. Given enough poverty, inequality, modernization, or ideological change, the social order will collapse and revolution will occur. Yet society is not a passive structure. Rather, societies consist of millions of active people and groups whose actions continually re-create and reinforce the social order.

Rulers provide defense and services in return for taxes; elites provide support for rulers in return for prestige and political and material rewards; and popular groups engage in economic activities, raise families, pray in churches, and receive protection in return for their economic activity and political obedience. The whole of society is continually being reconstituted by multiple overlapping relationships. These relationships allow societies to reproduce themselves over time while also being resilient, able to bounce back and reconstitute themselves after famines, wars, epidemics, local rebellions, religious heresies, and other crises. As long as elites remain united and loyal to the regime, and most popular groups remain reasonably content and focused on managing their own lives, regimes can be stable for centuries despite considerable strains and crises.

Revolutions as complex emergent processes

To understand what causes revolutions, it is also necessary to understand what keeps societies stable and resilient. In a stable society, popular groups engage in economic activities that generate sufficient income to support themselves and their families, and to pay the rents and taxes that support elites and the government. Elites—both those working for the government and those leading other organizations—act as the critical intermediaries between the state and the populace, organizing political, economic, religious and educational activities, reinforcing existing beliefs and behavior, and recruiting and training new elite members. The rulers provide rewards, recognition, and support to the elites, who in turn support the rulers' authority. Rulers also aim to protect the populace from banditry, invasions, famines, and other threats so that people can pay their rents and taxes. Under these conditions, a society is stable and resilient. It is resistant to the spread of rebellion and revolutionary ideologies because loyal military, bureaucratic and religious elites will suppress opposition, and because most groups are invested in the status quo and would not take major risks to change it.

Such a society can be described as being in "stable equilibrium." This concept comes from physical science. Imagine a ball sitting at the bottom of a large depression; if a small force moves the ball in any direction, it simply falls back into the depression, returning to its former state. Thus, a stable equilibrium is one in which the response to a moderate disturbance is a return to the original condition. Similarly, in a society in stable equilibrium, the response to a peasant revolt or strike, a war or economic crisis, is for rulers and elites and even most popular groups to act to restore the existing social order.

Yet consider what happens if the ball is not sitting in a depression, but resting on top of a hill. In the absence of any force the ball remains in place, but a small force pushing the ball now leads it to roll off the hill and head in a new direction. This is an unstable equilibrium—a small disturbance leads to an ever larger departure from the prior condition. This is precisely what happens to a society in a revolution.

When we examine societies in the years leading up to a revolution, we find that social relationships have changed. The rulers have become weakened, erratic, or predatory so that many of the elites no longer feel rewarded or supported, and are not inclined to support the regime. Elites are no longer unified but instead have become divided into mutually suspicious and distrusting factions. Popular groups find that their efforts are not providing them with expected rewards or outcomes. There may be shortages of land or work, excessive rents or falling real wages, and growing banditry, so that ordinary people are unsettled and distressed. Many elites and popular groups view the rulers and other elites as unjust; they are drawn to heterodox beliefs or ideologies that make sense of their grievances and offer solutions through social change. Rulers may attempt reforms, aiming to win elite or popular support and to gain additional resources. But these are usually too little and too late, and merely create more uncertainty and fresh opposition.

Under such conditions, a moderate or even small disturbance—a war, an economic crisis, a local rebellion, or an act of exceptional defiance or repression—can trigger spreading popular uprisings and heightened confrontations among elite groups. If a significant portion of the elites and diverse popular groups form a coalition against the rulers and demand major changes, a revolution has begun. If the military then suffers defections, and is reluctant or unable to overcome the spreading resistance, the revolution will succeed. This is how revolutions arise—over time, a society shifts from a condition of stable equilibrium to unstable equilibrium. Then even a small disorder can set off an accelerating movement toward greater disorder and the overturning of the existing regime.

Revolutions do not arise simply from mounting discontent over poverty, inequality, or other changes. Rather, revolution is a complex process that emerges from the social order becoming frayed in many areas at once.

Unstable equilibrium and the paradox of revolution

Unfortunately, it is not always easy to determine if a country is in unstable equilibrium, as despite underlying changes it may appear outwardly stable for a long time. Strikes, demonstrations, or revolts may be dismissed as insignificant as long as they are small and the military or police are willing and able to repress them. The degree to which other groups sympathize with protests, or that there is disaffection in the military and police, may not be visible until after it is too late. Elites may hide their growing discord and opposition until they seize the opportunity to act against the regime. Rulers may embark on reforms believing they will succeed, or undertake repressive acts believing they will end all opposition; it may not be clear until after the fact that reforms have failed to win support or that repression has triggered greater resentment and opposition.

Revolutions are thus like earthquakes. Geologists can identify major fault zones, and we know that earthquakes are most likely to arise in those zones. But a series of small tremors may be a release of tensions, or it may signify growing pressures that will soon produce a major shift; one cannot generally tell in advance. An earthquake may occur on a well-known fault, or it may erupt from a new or previously hidden fault line. Knowing the general mechanisms behind earthquakes has not allowed us to predict them. Similarly, social scientists can identify societies that seem to have major faults and growing tensions—these may be evident from signs of social conflict or heightened difficulties of institutions or groups carrying out accustomed tasks or meeting their goals. Yet that does not mean that we can predict exactly when a particular state will experience the shock of revolution.

Scholars of revolutions generally agree upon five elements that they consider necessary and sufficient to create an unstable social equilibrium from which revolutions can arise. First is national economic or fiscal strains; such conditions disrupt the flow of rents and taxes to rulers and elites and undermine the income of the general population. Such strains commonly lead rulers to increase taxes or borrow heavily, often in ways that seem unjust; they also hinder the rulers' ability to reward their supporters and pay their officials and military forces.

Second is growing alienation and opposition among the elites. Elites are always competing for position. Rivalries among families, parties, or factions are commonplace. However, a ruler usually can take advantage of this competition to win support from elites, playing off groups against each other and rewarding loyalty. Stable elites also manage to recruit and absorb talented newcomers. Alienation occurs when elite groups feel they are being systematically and unjustly excluded from favor. Older elites may feel they are being unfairly displaced by newcomers, or new aspiring elites may feel their way forward is being unfairly blocked. Elites may feel that a narrow group—a small circle of cronies or members of the rulers' ethnic or regional group—is unfairly getting a dominant share of political power or economic rewards. Under these conditions, elites can believe that their loyalty will not be rewarded, and that the existing regime will always work to their disadvantage. They may then seek reforms, or if those are blocked or considered ineffective, elites may seek to mobilize and even try to take advantage of popular discontent to put pressure on the regime for change. As their alienation grows, they may decide to overturn and replace the existing social order, rather than merely to improve their place within it.

Third, revolutionary mobilization builds on some form of increasingly widespread popular anger at injustice. This popular anger need not be the result of extreme poverty or inequality. Rather, what matters is that people feel they are losing their proper place in society for reasons that are not inevitable and not their fault. These may be peasants who worry that they are losing access to the land or being saddled with excessive rents or taxes or other burdens; workers who find themselves unable to find employment or who face rising prices for necessities and stagnant wages; students who cannot find the jobs they expect and desire; or mothers who feel they cannot provide for their children. When these groups feel their difficulties are the result of unjust actions by elites or rulers, they will take the risks of joining in revolts to call attention to their plight and demand change.

Popular groups may act through their own local organizations, such as peasant communes and village councils, workers' unions, neighborhoods, student or youth organizations, and guilds or professional groups. They may also be mobilized by elites, civil or military, who recruit and organize the populace to challenge the government.

Popular groups may engage in urban marches, demonstrations, and occupations of public spaces. In the nineteenth century, the call "to the barricades" was a call to erect barriers to keep state forces out of "liberated" neighborhoods; today an occupation is more likely to fill a central space with crowds, such as Tahrir Square in Cairo. Workers may also call for boycotts and general strikes. If the revolutionaries deem the government's forces too strong to challenge in the capital, they may instead organize guerrilla forces in remote mountainous or forested areas and seek to gradually build up their strength.

Rebellions that remain local and isolated are usually easily suppressed. But if rebellion spreads to many regions, and includes peasants, workers, and students, and these groups link up with elites, their resistance can become too extensive for government forces to deal with all at once. The revolutionary forces can then thrive in certain areas, evading government forces in some regions and striking in others. At some point, military officers or enlisted men may refuse to kill their own people to keep the government in power; at that point the defection or collapse of the military ushers in the victory of the revolutionary forces.

Fourth, bridging various popular and elite grievances and demands, and linking and mobilizing diverse groups, requires an ideology that presents a persuasive shared narrative of resistance. This may take the form of a new religious movement: fundamentalist religious groups, from English Puritanism to Jihadist Islam, have often justified revolt against an immoral ruler. It may take the form of a secular narrative against injustice, stressing the rights and the innocent victims that have been abused. It may be a narrative of nationalist liberation. Whatever their form, effective narratives of resistance highlight the terrible injustices of the current regime and create a sense of shared identity and righteousness among the opposition.

Although the elites may stress abstractions, such as the evils of capitalism or the importance of natural rights, the most effective narratives of resistance also draw on local traditions and stories of heroes who fought for justice in times past. American and French revolutionaries harked back to revolutionary episodes in ancient Greece and Rome. The Cuban and Nicaraguan Revolutions evoked the memory of earlier Cuban and Nicaraguan independence fighters, José Martí and Augusto César Sandino. Interestingly, research has shown that revolutionary ideologies need not provide a precise future plan to unite and motivate their followers. Rather, what works best are vague or utopian promises of better times ahead combined with a detailed and emotionally powerful depiction of the intolerable injustice and inescapable evils of the current regime.

Finally, a revolution requires favorable international relations. Revolutionary success has often depended on foreign support for the opposition coming at crucial times, or on the withdrawal of foreign support for the ruler. Conversely, many revolutions have failed or been reversed because of foreign intervention to support counterrevolution.

When these five conditions coincide—economic or fiscal strain, alienation and opposition among the elites, widespread popular anger at injustice, a persuasive shared narrative of resistance, and favorable international relations—the normal social mechanisms that restore order in crises are unlikely to work. Instead, societies where these conditions prevail are in an unstable equilibrium, where any untoward event can trigger escalating popular revolts and open elite resistance, producing a revolution.

Yet for all five of these conditions to coincide is rare. Moreover, they are difficult to assess accurately during periods of apparent stability. States may obfuscate their finances until they suddenly face bankruptcy; elites typically hide their disloyalty until they see an opportunity to act; and popular groups may seethe with inward anger but give few hints of how far they will go. Narratives of resistance may circulate discreetly underground or in hidden cells; whether other states will intervene to support or oppose a revolution is often unknown until the revolutionary struggle has begun.

The difficulty in determining whether outward stability represents a stable or unstable equilibrium produces the paradox of revolutions: In hindsight, after a revolution has occurred, it is quite apparent how severely the finances of governments and elites were affected by economic or fiscal strain; how much elites were alienated and divided from the regime; how widely felt were pangs of anger and injustice; how persuasive were the revolutionary narratives; and that international conditions were favorable. Indeed, it becomes possible to explain the origins of a revolution in such detail that its onset seems, in retrospect, inevitable. Yet at the same time, when revolutions do occur, they usually come as a complete shock to everyone, including the rulers, the revolutionaries themselves, and foreign powers. Lenin famously remarked in January 1917, just months before tsar's regime collapsed, that "We of the older generation may not live to see the decisive battles of this coming revolution."

This is because no one is usually positioned to be aware in advance of all five of these elements. Indeed rulers almost invariably underestimate how much they are seen as unjust or how much they have alienated elites; if they have a sense that things are amiss and embark on reforms they frequently make things worse. Revolutionaries often underestimate the fiscal weakness of the old regime or the magnitude of popular support for the opposition. They may believe they are in a struggle that will still last for years when elites and the military defect and the old regime suddenly collapses. That is why even though revolutions may seem inevitable in hindsight, they are usually seen as unlikely, even unimaginable, right up to the moment they actually occur.

Structural and transient causes of revolutions

These five conditions together constitute an unstable equilibrium. Yet they are not causes—they do not explain what caused the social order to fray at so many levels all at once. We still have to ask what kinds of events will produce a combination of fiscal decay, elite alienation, popular anger at injustice, the spread of narratives of resistance, and international support for revolutionary change.

Scholars typically differentiate between structural and transient causes. Structural causes are long-term and large-scale trends that undermine existing social institutions and relationships. Transient causes are contingent events, or actions by particular individuals or groups, that reveal the impact of longer term trends and often galvanize revolutionary oppositions to take further action.

One very common structural cause of revolutions is demographic change. For most of history, population has changed very slowly or has grown more slowly than economic and technical progress. Under those conditions, direct inheritance provides a very secure way of replacing rulers, reconstituting elites, and even assigning ordinary people to their jobs or professions. Yet when the population grows rapidly for several generations, the cumulating effects of population change can cause the institutions of social order to suffer. Land and jobs may grow scarce; rents rise and real wages decline, producing popular anger. Prices will rise but taxes may lag, making it more difficult for the ruler to reward supporters and pay the troops. As elites have more surviving children, inheritance no longer provides for them all, and competition for elite positions heats up. Finally, sustained population growth produces ever-larger youth cohorts—often described as a "youth bulge"—who find difficulty obtaining suitable jobs and are easily drawn to new ideologies and mobilized for social protest.

A second common structural cause is a shift in the pattern of international relations. Wars and international economic competition can weaken state authorities and empower new groups in society. Revolutions frequently arose in waves following global or continental wars, as happened in Europe after the Thirty Years War, in the decades after the Napoleonic Wars, in the wake of World Wars I and II, and at the conclusion of the Cold War.

Changing population patterns and shifts in international relations often affect many states in a region at the same time, creating a large number of states that are simultaneously moving into unstable equilibrium. If a triggering event occurs in one such state, then the outburst of revolution in that state can itself serve as the triggering event for revolutionary outbreaks in others. This is why revolutions have frequently occurred in waves that seem to spread rapidly from one apparently stable country to the next.

A third structural cause is uneven or dependent economic development. It is normal for economic development to initially create more equality as some regions or groups benefit most from the new technologies or economic organization. But all groups should benefit to some degree, and the laggards usually catch up as the new technology and economic patterns spread. Where economic growth is so uneven that the poor and even middle classes fall farther behind while a small elite grows rapidly richer; or where economic growth is so dependent on foreign investment that growth benefits mainly the foreign investors and their associates; then economic changes will be widely seen as unjust, creating popular grievances, and alienating and dividing the elites.

A fourth and related structural cause is new patterns of exclusion or discrimination against particular groups. Inequality is universal in human societies. However, ambitious individuals aspire to improve their own positions by military or educational or economic achievements, and most societies allow for a certain amount of mobility to absorb talented newcomers into the elite. Where entire groups face legal discrimination—such as commoners in societies with hereditary nobles, or ethnic or religious minorities that are excluded from politics and certain economic roles—the discrimination must be well established and consistent to be accepted as part of the normal order.

By contrast, new or differently enforced discrimination or exclusion can undermine the legitimacy of a regime and turn entire groups into enemies of the existing social order. If existing channels of social mobility are suddenly blocked; if new groups take power and exclude former elites; or if the numbers and wealth of a group increase greatly without any increased political opportunities for that group, then the existing equilibrium becomes unstable, as an entire social group becomes aggrieved and seeks to change the social system that they believe is unjustly holding them down.

A fifth structural cause is the evolution of personalist regimes. In many countries a leader who has come to power through an election, or as the head of a military regime or a party-state, becomes increasingly entrenched over time. By manipulating elites and political institutions to stay in power decade after decade, the ruler comes to see himself as the indispensable leader of the nation. Such rulers typically weaken or alienate the regular professional military and business elites, relying more and more on a small circle of family and cronies who obtain high positions and great wealth through personal favor. What had been an elected, military or party-based regime now becomes a personalist dictatorship.

In such regimes, the longer the ruler remains in power the more corrupt their regime becomes, as family members and cronies take greater advantage of their positions. The ruler may lose touch and not care if the bulk of the population suffers from his economic policies. As more elite and popular groups feel excluded and estranged, they come to view the regime as illegitimate and unjust. Should an economic crisis weaken the ruler or spur revolt, such rulers may quickly find themselves isolated and deserted by their elites.

Both personalist dictators and traditional monarchies often fall victim to the combination of structural causes known as "the dictator's dilemma." The ruler of a relatively poor or backward nation often must invest heavily in upgrading its military and economic capacity to keep up with military and economic pressures from more advanced states. Doing so requires creating a more educated and professional military and civil service, encouraging private enterprise, increasing enrollments in schools and universities, and expanding cities and communications. It may also involve inviting extensive foreign investment.

But unless these processes are carefully managed, they can cause social relationships to fray. Better educated professionals, students, and private businessmen will resent the power and favoritism of a venal dictator, the privileges of entrenched elites, and the benefits going to foreign interests. Older elites may try to block the progress of newcomers. Growing private enterprises may displace peasants from their lands and compete with traditional craft workers. Expanded urban populations are more difficult to control and become centers for the spread of alternative ideologies. Modernizing dictatorships and monarchies thus lay the basis for a vigorous opposition to their rule; if they falter in the face of war or economic crises, or have fallen into patterns of blatant corruption and exclusionary rule, they are ripe for revolution.

In contrast to these structural causes, which gradually create unstable equilibrium over years or decades, transient causes are sudden events that push a society out of stability. These may include spikes in inflation, particularly of food prices; defeat in war; and riots or demonstrations that challenge state authority. In addition, state responses to protest can trigger wider protests. When most people see protestors as extremists, and they are isolated targets of state action, repression is usually effective. But when protestors are seen as ordinary members of society, then repression that is too broad or inconsistent can inflame elite and popular perceptions of the regime as dangerous, illegitimate, and unjust.

These transient events are indeed causes of revolutions, since in unstable states they lead people to turn against the state more openly and in larger numbers, or weaken the state's ability to defend itself and hasten elite defections. Yet the very same events occur in dozens of states each year without producing revolutions, because those states have the resilience to restore social order in the face of crises. It is therefore the structural causes, which create the underlying instability, that scholars treat as the fundamental causes of revolutions.

Once a regime has been weakened, key elites have defected, and revolutionaries at the head of armies or popular revolts have seized power, a revolution has begun. Yet how events will end is still undetermined, for revolutions are long processes, not simple events. They may veer through counterrevolution, civil war, terror, and renewed revolutionary episodes before achieving stability. And their outcomes may range from democracy to renewed dictatorship.

Chapter 3
Revolutionary processes, leaders, and outcomes

Many observers of revolutions focus on their origins—what caused popular uprisings, and why did the old regime fall? Yet the fall of the old regime merely begins the drama of revolution. As revolutions unfold, revolutionary leaders gain success or are cast aside as new ones emerge. Repeated upheavals and civil wars often arise as groups struggle for power and seek to build new institutions. The outcomes of revolutions are never given just from their origins; they are forged in the process of revolution itself.

The process of revolution

A revolution begins when the government loses control of a portion of its population and territory to groups demanding a change of government to rectify injustices. The area controlled by the opposition may be as small as a public square in a capital or regional city, or as distant as a mountain redoubt on the far edge of the country.

Most such beginnings lead to swift repression, or years of futile and insignificant activity. However, if a country is already in an unstable equilibrium, with the state facing economic or fiscal problems, a restive population, and declining loyalty among officials and elites, then such small beginnings soon lead to the loss of ever more territory and population to the opposition.

This is the first phase of revolution: state breakdown, when the state loses control of society. Although no two revolutions unfold in exactly the same way, scholars have identified two main patterns of state breakdown—central collapse and peripheral advance.

In cases of central collapse, the regime has already weakened greatly, usually far more than is evident. The government may be nearly bankrupt; it has been losing legitimacy with business, administrative, and military elites for some time; and popular groups have been mounting local protests, strikes, or rural revolts in recent years. Such revolutions may start with peasant revolts or uprisings in rural areas, with urban demonstrations, or with an elite challenge to state authority. They may be precipitated by a short-term economic downturn or price spike, a military defeat, a manipulated election, or new and resented actions by the government. Whatever the initial impetus, it is swiftly followed by a major demonstration in the capital city.

The government tries to disperse the demonstration but encounters surprising difficulty in doing so; initial efforts by the government are followed by expanding demonstrations. Police forces are unable to cope with the urban disorders, and the government faces a situation where the military has to be called in. Yet the military refuses to act decisively to clear the streets; key units may stand aside while others may even defect and go over to the opposition. The inaction of the military acts as a signal to the ruler, elites, and the population that the regime is defenseless. Crowds surge and take over the capital; similar mass demonstrations spread to other cities and the countryside. All of this generally unfolds over a few weeks or at most a few months. The ruler may then flee or be captured, while elites supported by crowds or the military take over government buildings and set up a provisional government. Examples include the French and Russian Revolutions, the European Revolutions of 1848, the Iranian Islamic Revolution, the East German and Romanian anticommunist Revolutions, the "color revolutions" in the Philippines and Ukraine, and the Arab Revolutions of 2011 in Tunisia and Egypt.

In cases of peripheral advance, the decay of the old regime is less advanced. Yet a group of elites seeking to overturn the government is able to establish a foothold in some part of the country, usually a mountainous or forested area remote from the capital. This rural base may remain small and insignificant for years. If the regime is becoming more unstable—weakening economically, suffering military reversals, losing legitimacy with additional popular groups, losing the loyalty of additional elites—the opposition nucleus grows as it acquires new supporters, while support for the existing government declines. The rebels may adopt guerrilla warfare, melting into the countryside and striking periodically at government forces, or staging spectacular raids designed to demonstrate the weakness of the government. Workers may strike in support of the rebels.

Eventually, the opposition develops into a conventional army capable of fighting a civil war to take the capital city. Or the rebels may pursue nonviolent tactics using ever larger popular demonstrations, strikes, and boycotts to press the government to cede power. Either way, external powers may play a key role. If other nations or groups help arm and organize the opposition, or if former external allies withdraw their support for the ruler, the balance of power can start to shift decisively in favor of the opposition. As the balance tips against the regime, government forces will suffer defections and further declines in morale and military effectiveness. This process usually takes years, sometimes more than a decade. Yet at the end, as the old regime's force crumble or retreat, the revolutionary forces take the capital and establish a new regime. Examples include the American Revolution, the Chinese Communist Revolution, the Cuban Revolution, the Indian Independence Movement, the

Nicaraguan Revolution, and the Arab Revolution of 2011
in Libya.

In recent years, a third and novel pattern—the negotiated
revolution—has emerged. These may start like central collapse or
peripheral advance revolutions, with mass demonstrations in the
capital or the opposition gaining control of local bases. But instead
of the ruler fleeing and ceding power to a provisional revolutionary
government, or being driven out by a civil war, the authorities
recognize that they cannot overcome the opposition and instead
seek to negotiate the entry of the opposition into a new, joint
regime. This may involve new elections in which both the ruling
and opposition parties seek seats in the legislature, or joint councils
with members of the opposition and the old regime leadership.
However, the overwhelming popular support for the revolutionary
party allows them to dominate the new institutions, win control
of the government, and enact laws to reshape the political and
economic order. Examples include the South African anti-apartheid
revolution (which arose from bases in the Black townships), the
Polish Solidarity revolution (whose bases were in the shipyards and
the Catholic Church), and the Czechoslovak "velvet" revolution.

Whether a revolutionary government comes to power with
surprising speed in the capital, or it advances to win power
through a lengthy struggle to expand its base and displace the
regime, seizing power is just the first phase of the revolutionary
process. At first, the fall of the old regime is greeted with jubilation.
A "revolutionary honeymoon" period of a few weeks ensues in
which people enjoy an unfamiliar taste of freedom, go out of their
way to demonstrate solidarity and friendship with fellow citizens,
and exhibit enormous optimism for the future. The initial elections
under the new regime are usually greeted with great excitement
and an outpouring of new parties and political groups.

Yet a number of critical decisions soon need to be made by the
revolutionary government. How will leaders be chosen and what

laws will govern the exercise of power? Will power be centralized or dispersed to regional and local authorities? Who will control the military? These issues could be determined by a series of decrees or laws, but often involve drafting and adopting a new constitution.

Other issues must also be settled. What will be the new regime's relations to other states—will it seek new allies or continue to fight the old regime's opponents? Will there be a redistribution of property or a change in the state religion? How will the new government finance its operations—by old taxes or new ones, by seizure of property or sale of state assets? How will the remaining leaders and supporters of the old regime be treated? What new rules should guide the economy, education, the media, public services, or the role of minorities? And if the old regime was facing financial or military or economic crises, what measures will the new regime take to address them?

These questions are so wide ranging and so important that the diverse groups who made the revolution can rarely agree on them. If the old regime's supporters have mostly fled and no pressing external threats are present, the revolutionary leaders may be able to work out their differences peacefully, spend time negotiating a constitution that can win wide support, and develop a sharing or alternation in power among different groups. But this is rare; more commonly disagreements over these pressing major issues create cleavages among different groups. The revolution then enters the phase of postrevolutionary power struggles.

These splits are often exacerbated by crises that threaten the new regime. Supporters of the old order, often with support from foreign powers, may try to unseat the new regime through counter-revolution. Regional groups or minorities may fight for more power or against revolutionary polices. These disruptions may cause inflation or economic collapse. Civil or international war may follow. Revolutionary leaders often will sharply divide over how to respond to such crises.

In the course of this polarization, moderate and radical factions frequently form. Moderate factions may want to continue certain features or policies of the old regime, and shrink from drastic changes in economic or social organization. Yet if war, economic crisis, or counterrevolution threatens the new regime, moderate measures often will not suffice. Should moderate policies fail, moderate leaders will be discredited and popular support will shift to radicals promising to bring better results by more extreme measures. Ruthless actions to raise revenues and forces to defend the new regime, to redistribute property, and harsh actions to deal with internal and external enemies become the order of the day.

These conflicts usually play out in ideological terms as well, with radical leaders claiming to be the "true voices" of the people and the revolution, while tarring moderates and opponents as reactionaries and traitors. Earlier constitutions may be discarded and replaced by more radical documents; many revolutions go through numerous short-lived constitutions. New symbols and ceremonies, new forms of address (e.g., "citizen" and "comrade") new official titles, changes in administrative units and capitals, and new forms of art, dress, and language are commonly promoted by the new regime.

Radical groups often displace the moderates through a coup or insurrection, seizing power and taking over the revolutionary government. Demanding loyalty to their vision and policies, they may turn to purges or terror, executing and imprisoning many thousands. Often, revolutionaries will turn on each other, exiling or executing former comrades. Danton, Trotsky, Zapata, Lin Biao, Bani-Sadr, and Escalante are just a few of the once-prominent revolutionary leaders who were sacrificed to the gods of revolution by their colleagues.

Even after the radicals are securely in power, their new policies may bring economic disorder or provoke civil and international wars, which cause thousands or even millions of deaths. Other nations may fear the radical revolutionaries' attempts to spread their vision and policies abroad; or they may think the disorder of revolution makes the new regime vulnerable to military defeat. Either way, the likelihood is very high that revolutionary regimes will soon be involved in international conflicts.

At some point, the radicals defeat their enemies or are defeated themselves. The new government then needs to be institutionalized so that people can return to work and the economy be restored. Whether it is the radicals and their heirs or new moderate rulers who succeed to power, the revolutionary regime becomes the "new normal" government. People adopt ordinary careerism rather than ideologically driven passion as their approach to politics, and the government seeks a stable place in the international order as a great or regional power. After this phase of consolidation, things settle down and the revolution appears to be over.

Yet after another decade or two, the older radicals or a new generation may feel that this new order is failing to live up to the ideals of the revolution. They may seek to mobilize elite and popular groups for a new set of revolutionary measures, attacking existing officials and their policies, and seeking more radical economic and political changes. This second radical phase usually does not overturn the revolutionary government but revives its radicalism, which can lead to major new departures in domestic and international policies, and new waves of popular mobilization and conflict. This second radical phase is usually the final burst of revolutionary energy; whether it prevails or is defeated, what follows is a reconsolidated, stable version of the revolutionary regime. Examples include Stalin's collectivization campaign in the 1930s, Mao's Cultural Revolution in the 1960s, and Lázaro Cárdenas's nationalizations and land reforms in Mexico in the 1930s.

Revolutionary leadership: visionary and organizational

Revolutionary leaders are the pivots of history, the figures through which we come to see revolutions. In their own countries, they often are lionized as "fathers of the nation" and can become the subject of personality cults. Some—Washington, Napoleon, Lenin—have gone down in history as heroes who created powerful new nations. Others—Robespierre, Stalin, Mao—have gone down in history as monsters who blindly pursued their ideologies and were responsible for the deaths of thousands or millions. To be accurate, many revolutionary leaders were a bit of both.

Because in hindsight the many factors leading nations to enter unstable equilibrium can appear overwhelming, the role of revolutionary leaders is sometimes minimized. When it seems that the old order was bound to collapse, revolutionary leaders simply emerge to pick up the pieces. Yet it requires skillful revolutionary leadership to take advantage of instability and disorder, and to construct from this chaos a successful revolutionary movement and build a new regime. In the absence of revolutionary leaders to articulate and spread a new vision of society, an economic crisis or military defeat will likely be followed by the restoration of the old order with just a few institutional tweaks and adjustments. If revolutionary leaders are not able to weave coalitions across various elite and popular groups to build a durable coalition, the old regime will likely defeat its enemies and no revolution will occur. The decisions to pursue moderate or radical policies, to enter into war or terror, how to restructure law and society, and the ultimate success and outcomes of revolutions are thus driven by revolutionary leaders.

Moderate revolutionary leaders are generally found within the ranks of the existing elite and often even within the existing regime. They may be military officers or legislators or regional officials. Frequently they are advocates of reform, and only

Revolutionary processes, leaders, and outcomes

33

reluctantly pursue revolution when it appears that the old regime is intransigent, erratic, or incompetent to meet pressing challenges to the nation. Radical revolutionary leaders are also usually drawn from the ranks of the existing elites but from a more middling stratum of junior officers, professionals, university students, and local leaders. They are the same people, in terms of their background and upbringing, who in more stable times would pursue careers in politics or business or the professions. They generally have a radicalizing experience—they or a family member may have been abused by a government official, or they may have been punished for their political views. They tend to be fiercely patriotic and to have an unusually acute awareness of the problems in their society leading to unstable equilibrium, thus devoting extensive time and effort to developing solutions and campaigning for major changes in government policies—campaigns that often get them into trouble with the authorities.

Revolutionary leadership requires two distinct kinds of skills. Visionary leaders are prolific writers, and often great speechmakers, who articulate the faults of the old society and make a powerful case for social change. They create a portrait of the injustices of the old regime and of the absolute necessity and inevitability of change that is capable of motivating and uniting diverse groups to support the revolution. During the revolution, visionary leaders continue to inspire and guide the revolutionary forces. Such visionary leaders include Thomas Jefferson, Robespierre, Francisco Madero, V. I. Lenin, Mao Zedong, Fidel Castro, Ho Chi Minh, Mahatma Gandhi, Vaclav Havel, and Ayatollah Khomeini.

Organizational leaders are great organizers and leaders of organizations; it is they who organize revolutionary armies and bureaucracies and make sure that they are paid and supplied. The organizational leaders figure out how to realize the ideas of visionary leaders, to make sure that the revolution can defeat its enemies and meet its economic and political goals. They tend to be pragmatic and are often skilled military generals. Such organizational leaders include George Washington, Napoleon, Venustiano Carranza, Leon Trotsky, Zhou Enlai, Raoul Castro, Vo Nguyen Giap and Lech Wałęsa.

Successful revolutions require both kinds of leadership. Without visionary leaders to inspire and unite the opposition, the existing regime can usually isolate and defeat its fragmented opponents. Without organizational leaders, the revolutionary forces will easily be defeated by their opponents, either internal or external, as the new revolutionary regime decays and falls apart due to ineffective policies and lack of resources.

Most revolutions exhibit visionary and organizational leaders operating as partners; indeed they may have several leaders taking visionary and organizational roles. But in some cases, a single figure acts as both the visionary and organizational leader; notable examples include Simon Bolivar, Kemal Ataturk, and Deng Xiaoping. Whatever their role, how revolutionary leaders are viewed is often determined by the outcomes of the revolutions they led.

Revolutionary outcomes

It is often difficult to determine the outcome of a revolution, as it is hard to know when the outcome should be assessed. Is the major outcome of the Russian Revolution of 1917 the millions killed by Stalin's collectivization campaigns in 1930s? Or should we focus on the remarkable survival of the Soviet Union after the Nazi onslaught and its rise to become one of the world's two superpowers by the 1960s? Should the collapse of the Soviet Union in 1989–1991 be viewed as the inevitable outcome of the Russian Revolution seventy-two years earlier, or instead as the result of the poor choices of Gorbachev and other Soviet leaders in the 1980s?

Is the outcome of the American Revolution of 1776 the Constitution adopted in 1787, which has lasted for more than two hundred years? Or was the outcome of the Revolution and the compromises in the Constitution the collapse of the United States into bloody civil war in the 1860s?

The outcomes of revolutions are many and varied, and appear on different timescales. The American Revolution is hailed for creating a democracy; yet in fact more than half the population (women and slaves) was denied the vote for more than a hundred years. At the time of the Proletarian Cultural Revolution, China seemed to be torn apart and impoverished by internal conflict and ideological discord; twenty years later China was well on its way to achieving a modern miracle of growth and becoming the world's second largest economy.

Despite this variety, there are a few established principles regarding revolutionary outcomes. First, outcomes do not emerge quickly. The processes described in the previous section typically take years or even decades to unfold. Ten to twelve years is the average time from the fall of the old regime before the features of the stable new revolutionary regime are clear.

Second, revolutions fall into several types with characteristic outcomes. "Social Revolutions" involve the redistribution of large amounts of property and bring members of previously excluded social groups to power. Because of the great changes involved, they invariably invite efforts at counterrevolution and require a powerful regime to consolidate change. They therefore produce highly centralized, authoritarian states, often party-states or communist regimes. They generally introduce social programs, such as land redistribution or collectivization, literacy and educational reforms, and public health measures aimed at establishing greater economic equality. They often experience a burst of rapid industrialization and economic growth due to the strong direction of the central regime, but this growth weakens substantially and leads to economic stagnation unless market-oriented reforms are introduced. Examples include the

French, Mexican, Russian, Chinese Communist, Cuban, Ethiopian, and Iranian Islamic Revolutions.

"Anticolonial Revolutions" involve rebellion against foreign powers that control a territory in order to create a newly independent nation. Except for creating independence, they have uncertain outcomes in the domestic sphere—some have led to democracies, some to military regimes or civilian dictatorships, others to communist regimes. The common characteristic of their outcomes is that the appearance of new nations disrupts the prevailing system of international relations. The loss of territory often weakens the former colonial power, while the new states may become regional powers in their own right. Other powers may seek to improve their positions by seeking an alliance with the new states or trying to control them. As a result, anticolonial revolutions almost always produce a major alteration of international relations. Since shifts in the international system affect many states, if the colonial regimes of other states have also entered an unstable equilibrium, then one anticolonial revolution can trigger a wave of such revolutions across a continent. Examples include the American, Haitian, Latin American, Algerian, Indian, Vietnamese, Indonesian, Angolan, and Mozambique revolutions.

"Democratizing" revolutions seek to overturn an authoritarian regime that has grown corrupt, ineffective, and illegitimate, and replace it with a more accountable and representative regime. They do not mobilize supporters on the basis of class antagonisms (peasants vs. landlords, workers vs. capitalists) but rather draw support from across the social spectrum. They may begin with an election campaign or with protests against fraudulent elections. They lack the ideological fervor of revolutions whose leaders see themselves as creating a new social order or a new nation; they are therefore usually nonviolent and do not lead to civil war, nor to a radical phase, nor revolutionary terror. Unfortunately, the lack of severe contestation means that government passes into the hands of a mixture of groups, none of which wishes to take the ruthless measures necessary to consolidate power and strengthen the new regime. These revolutions thus often drift; leaders fall into corruption and petty infighting, and the eventual outcome is a usually a flawed democracy with either frequent shifts in leadership or recurrent authoritarian tendencies. This is especially true where countries lack previous experience with democracy. Examples include the European Revolutions of 1848; the Chinese Republican Revolution of 1911; the anticommunist revolution in the Soviet Union; the "color revolutions" in Ukraine, the Philippines, and Georgia; and the 2011 Arab Revolutions in Tunisia and Egypt.

Not all revolutions fall into one of these major types. The 2011 Revolutions in Libya and Syria, for example, began as democratizing revolutions but the tenacity of ethnic or tribal loyalties to the rulers led to civil war. The Turkish Revolution, the Meiji Restoration, and the Nasser Revolution in Egypt all sought to replace traditional monarchies or empires with modern national states with constitutions and secular governments; but all led eventually to military regimes.

Revolutions are most likely to lead to democracy in societies that have prior experience with democracy, and where the revolutions do not provoke strong counterrevolutionary threats that trigger civil wars. Conversely, the greater the degree of polarization and conflict among contending groups within the new regime, and the greater the attachment of revolutionary leaders to a particular ideology or ethnic identity, the less likely is a democratic outcome.

Attachment to a particular ideology or ethnic identity makes new revolutionary regimes particularly harsh on minorities, who often are scapegoated for social problems and singled out as traitors or enemies of the new regime. In some cases, such as the Nazi Revolution in Germany and the Khmer Revolution in Cambodia, assaults by the new regime on minorities have reached the level of genocide. Racial and religious minorities may be promised much, but postrevolutionary societies rarely deliver true equality. For example, Blacks in communist Cuba, as well as in the United States after emancipation, continued to experience discrimination despite formal proclamations of equality.

One other area in which revolutionary outcomes have consistently disappointed their followers is women's rights. Throughout history, women have marched, demonstrated, and fought alongside men for social justice. In 1789 the women of Paris marched on Versailles to demand food and dignity for their families and children, while in 1791 Marie Gouze published the *Declaration of the Rights of Woman*. In Mexico, Dolores Jiménez y Muro and Hermila Galindo were leading political organizers and writers, while thousands of women fought as *soldaderas* in the revolutionary armies. In Russia and Germany, Alexandra Kollontai, Nadezhda Krupskaya, and Rosa Luxembourg helped lead the communist and socialist parties. In Cuba Celia Sánchez and Vilma Espín played key roles in the revolution, and in Nicaragua more than 30 percent of the armed Sandinistas were women.

In return for their exemplary courage and sacrifices, revolutionary leaders frequently promise equal roles for women in the new revolutionary regime. Yet without exception to date, once the revolutionary regime takes power, men seize most of the major political, military, and economic leadership posts, while women are encouraged to return to their families and focus on domestic duties. Even where women are given opportunities to gain educations and enter work and the professions, their pay remains worse, and they still bear the greatest burden for raising children and maintaining homes. While in a few cases women have emerged from revolutions as the leaders of their nation—such as Indira Gandhi in India, Violeta Chamorro in Nicaragua, and Corazon Aquino in the Philippines—they have done so as the heirs of politically prominent fathers or husbands, and have been unable to shift the dominant patriarchal character of their societies. Alongside ethnic and religious minorities, women have consistently been let down by revolutionary promises for equality. They have made progress only where they have undertaken their own mass campaigns for the right to vote and women's rights.

Revolutionary processes and outcomes have evolved throughout history. The idea of citizenship, born in the revolutions of ancient Greek city-states, was revived in the Renaissance and then fueled revolutions in America and France in the eighteenth century. The dream of socialism emerged in the nineteenth century and shaped communist revolutions around the world in the nineteenth and twentieth centuries. The European notion of nationalism as the right of ethnic communities to govern themselves later produced anticolonial revolutions against European powers. In sum, revolutions have constantly revised and reconstituted politics, nations, and international relations.

If not for revolutions, we would not have today's world of democratic and constitutional governments, campaigns for liberty and human rights, or our concepts of citizenship and nationalism. Yet the costs have been stark—in the French Revolution more than a million French men and women died in the uprisings and revolutionary civil and international wars, roughly one in twenty of the prerevolutionary population. Many tens of millions perished in the Mexican, Russian, and Chinese Communist Revolutions, roughly one in ten of these countries' peoples. Some recent revolutions have been less bloody, such as the "velvet" revolutions against Communism in Eastern Europe. But against these we must place events such as the Khmer Rouge Revolution in Cambodia, in which nearly 30 percent of the population died in war and genocide. Revolutions thus deserve their reputation for horror as well as heroism.

Chapter 4
Revolutions in the ancient world

Revolutions are nearly as old as history itself. Ever since we have had records of government and taxation—as long ago as the pharaohs of Egypt—there have been efforts to overthrow governments in the name of greater social justice and to replace one set of government institutions with different ones. But as governments changed their character, so too did revolutions. Even the understanding of what revolution entailed—by both revolutionaries and political theorists—has developed over time. In different eras, the term "revolution" has meant a circular pattern of political changes, the restoration of natural order, violent and permanent political change, and today has come to include the peaceful assertion of democratic rights.

Revolutions from the pharaohs to Greece and Rome

The reign of Pepi II, the last pharaoh of the Old Kingdom in Egypt, appears to have ended in a revolution in the twenty-second century BCE. The pharaoh was losing control to regional lords, and as central rule weakened, people attacked the homes of the wealthy and seized their possessions. Magistrates were driven from their offices and palaces plundered. An ancient papyrus scroll describing this event relates how amid famine and destruction, the social order was overturned: "The poor man is full of joy. Every town says: 'Let us suppress the powerful among us.'... The son of a man of rank is no long distinguished from him who has no such father. . . . Behold, the possessors of robes are [now] in rags [while] He who begged for himself his dregs [has] bowls full to overflowing. . . . The King has been taken away by poor men." Local oligarchies took over and ruled for more than a hundred years, until a new pharaoh established the first dynasty of the Middle Kingdom. During the Egyptian revolution of 2011, Egyptians proudly retold this story of the world's first known popular revolution to show that Egyptians had a long history of challenging injustice.

Archeologists have also found evidence of attacks on palaces in the eastern Mediterranean in the thirteenth century BCE, but it is uncertain if these were marauders or revolutions. However, by the eighth century BCE in Greece, we find indisputable cases of conflict leading to constitutional changes.

Up to about 800 BCE, the cost of bronze arms and chariots was so great that only aristocrats could afford them. Kings backed by aristocrats and priests were dominant. Indeed in Egypt, Persia and elsewhere, rulers claimed divine or semidivine status. Popular mobilization to change the nature of government was quite rare.

As populations grew, trade increased and weapons became more affordable. Heavily armed infantry (hoplites) replaced aristocratic charioteers as the core of armies. This undermined the aristocrats' dominance, and Greek societies began to experience organized conflict between elite and popular groups. These conflicts produced periodic shifts in power, several of which led to major changes in government institutions. For the first time in history, from roughly 700 BCE to 100 CE, revolutions became fairly common.

The Greeks recognized five main forms of government: monarchy, in which a royal family claimed hereditary rights to rule; aristocracy, in which a privileged elite held power; tyranny, which we would call dictatorship, in which an individual gains power by force and rules in arbitrary fashion; oligarchy, in which a small group of citizens (usually the richest) makes the laws and decisions for all; and democracy, in which all active male citizens join in making the laws and passing judgments, and in choosing their leaders. Both Plato and Aristotle observed this variety of governments across Greece and wrote about the causes of changes in regimes.

For both Plato and Aristotle, the cause of revolutions was social injustice. Plato argued that the best society is ruled by an aristocracy based on merit and virtue; but when aristocracies focus on money instead of virtue, they become ineffective, rival-torn oligarchies, and will be overthrown by the people. The latter would create a democracy; but a democracy in turn is likely to degenerate as everyone pursues their own interests. Eventually this disorder opens the way for a tyrant to seize power. Aristotle identified many different causes that could lead to revolution, including personal rivalries and external interventions. But the primary cause was always injustice—either the wealthy few oppressing the poorer majority or the poorer majority making demagogic attacks on the rich. For Aristotle stability depended on having a constitution that maintained a balance of wealth, numbers, and merit.

In practice, many Greek city-states underwent a series of revolutions as popular and oligarchic factions fought for power. These revolutions often arose in the wake of wars, particularly when military defeat weakened the ruling party. A common pattern was for aristocrats to be overthrown by a populist leader who became a tyrant. Then the tyrant would be overthrown by a popular movement, which produced a formal constitution, seeking to create a more balanced, law-based form of government. The constitutions of Solon for Athens and of Lycurgus for Sparta were the best-known models, both relying on an assembly of male citizens to make the laws.

During the Peloponnesian Wars, when Athens and Sparta vied for power across Greece, they often fomented revolutions, seeking to overturn governments allied to their rival (much like the United States and the Soviet Union during the modern Cold War). The great ancient historian of these wars, Thucydides, showed how much of Greece was convulsed by revolutions in this period. In Book 3 of *The History of the Peloponnesian War* he describes in detail the revolution in Corcyra (427 BCE), in which the pro-Athenian democratic faction (which freed the slaves to fight on their behalf) fought against the pro-Spartan oligarchic faction (which hired mercenaries to fight for them). Thucydides reports that much like the great revolutions that came in later centuries, the revolution in Corcyra was characterized by butchery and chaos—"Death thus raged in every shape, and as usually happens at such times, there was no length to which violence did not go." The revolt ended when Athens sent a large fleet to Corcyra, and the democratic faction massacred its rivals.

The glories of Rome also have their roots in an ancient revolution. It appears that the city-state of Rome was initially ruled by foreign Etruscan kings. At the end of the sixth century BCE the Romans rose up and expelled the last foreign king, replacing the monarchy with a citizen-based government, which they called a republic. This term came from the Latin "res publica" or "public affairs," indicating that politics were now a public concern, not a private matter for kings and nobles. This revolution produced a regime in which an aristocratic Senate advised the state and proposed laws, but all citizens voted in assemblies that elected the major officials—the consuls and tribunes—and passed the laws.

The Roman Republic lasted roughly five hundred years in this form. But as the Republic's conquests grew, and the population and land under control of the city increased, it became more difficult for the institutions designed for citizens to participate in government to function. Immense wealth accrued to the leading

1. The Senate meeting in Rome.

senators and immense power to leaders of the army. The Senate had increasing difficulty controlling the leading generals, and the people lost faith in the Senate. In the late second century BCE the Gracchus brothers, Tiberius and Gaius, who were tribunes elected by the Plebian Council, tried to pass laws that would redistribute some of the wealth of the patricians to the common people. Sometimes lauded as history's first socialists, they were assassinated for their troubles, and their efforts failed.

The leading generals then sought to win popular support for their challenges to the Senate. In 49 BCE, after a series of military victories abroad that gained him great fame and popularity, Julius Caesar defied the Senate's attempt to relieve him of his command and instead took his army to Rome. He spent the next five years warring against his opponents, conquering Egypt (and its queen, Cleopatra), and having the Senate grant him more extensive and permanent powers. In 44 BCE, as told by Plutarch and Shakespeare, he was assassinated by a group of Senators who feared his growing power.

After his death, his nephew Octavian, drawing on the enormous popularity of Caesar with the people and soldiers of Rome, undertook a series of civil wars to defeat all of his uncle's enemies. When Octavian gained sole power, in what is now commonly called "The Roman Revolution," he completed the work of degrading the powers of the Senate and Assemblies, and created the political framework for the Roman Empire.

Octavian adopted the name Augustus Caesar. Although he permitted the Senate and Assemblies to exist, he increasingly had himself portrayed as having divine attributes, thus putting his decisions above any other laws or institutions. He took control of the selection of military and civilian officials, placing trusted kin and loyalists in key positions. The new imperial system lay the groundwork for almost two thousand years in which all Roman emperors, Byzantine emperors, and later the kings of Europe would claim a "divine right" to rule.

The Roman religion at the time of Augustus followed the Greeks in having many gods, so that taking on divine attributes made Augustus just another one of the many descendants of the Olympians who had been heroes or demigods on earth. However, when Christianity came to the empire, the one true God and his son Jesus Christ were considered to have given their divine authority to kings to rule over humanity as their earthly regents. This placed kings above any man-made laws and made rebellion against a duly-anointed king an act of heresy, not merely political conflict. As a result, people became subjects rather than citizens, and revolutions went into abeyance for more than a thousand years.

Revolutions in abeyance under emperors and kings, 1 CE–1200 CE

Ancient Greece and Italy were not rich areas—mountainous and swampy peninsulas, they lacked the vast river valleys and plains that had been the foundation for wealthy empires in Egypt,

Mesopotamia, Persia, northern India, and China. Whereas the city-states of Greece and Rome thus developed as small, fairly egalitarian societies that experienced revolutions and developed constitutions and the concept of citizenship, no similar developments took place in other major civilizations. Indeed, wherever vast empires arose, government took the form of a divinely sanctioned hereditary ruler wielding enormous wealth and power through an appointed bureaucracy of powerful officials, usually in close cooperation with a hierarchy of religious priests. Such bureaucratic-agrarian empires often experienced peasant uprisings and regional rebellions, but underwent dynastic cycles rather than experiencing revolutions.

In these empires, a ruling family would periodically encounter difficulty maintaining their rule. As with Pepi II, local lords might gain power at the expense of the central regime. Or the overall economy would experience a period of difficulty due to sustained population increase; the resulting scarcity of land would make it more difficult for peasants to feed their families, and for elites and the imperial government to sustain their revenues. Elites then would call for reform and would usually claim that an unjust ruler was responsible for their ills. Yet such empires generally held to an ideal of a golden past associated with the founding era or sacred books of their civilization. So when injustice, popular suffering, and administrative crises arose, the diagnosis was always that the ruler had departed from the traditional virtues of the past. In China, the phrase was that the ruler had "lost the mandate of Heaven" for failing to conform to Confucian virtues. An uprising against the government that produced a new ruler therefore usually led to administrative reforms designed to make the new government a more efficient version of the older, idealized model. A new dynasty would thus arise, but its political institutions would simply be a somewhat reformed version of those of the previous regime.

This was the pattern that prevailed in the Hellenistic kingdoms, which arose in the eastern Mediterranean and central Asia after

Philip of Macedon and Alexander the Great had extinguished the independence of the Greek city-states and created a vast empire. It was the pattern in Islamic civilization, including Persia, the Arab caliphate and the Islamic dynasties of North Africa and Spain, and the Turkish Ottoman Empire. Indeed, the fourteenth-century Arab sociologist Ibn Khaldun was the first scholar to detail a theory of dynastic cycles. It was also the pattern of classical India, of the Byzantine Empire in the eastern Mediterranean, and of Imperial China. And it also became the pattern in Europe under the Roman Empire from the time of Augustus.

There were a few exceptions wherein a shift of dynastic control from one ruling family to another did have the character of a revolution, with a fight for greater justice producing a new pattern of regime authority or new groups rising to power. Two of these still influence modern-day politics.

One was the struggle in the early Islamic Empire known as the "Abbasid Revolution." After the death of the Prophet Muhammad in 632 CE, his followers chose the head of the Muslim community, the caliph. Under the early caliphs, Islam spread across the Middle East. The fourth caliph was Ali, Muhammad's first cousin and son-in-law, and closest living relative. However, in 661 CE Ali was assassinated. After his death, power was claimed by the governor of Syria, who founded the Umayyad dynasty. Over the next century, the Umayyad caliphs expanded Islamic control from Spain to Persia. Yet they faced many revolts, most notably by the followers of Ali. These partisans (in Arabic, *shi'a*) of Ali claimed that the caliphate should remain in direct descent from the prophet, and thus that the Umayyad caliphs were not legitimate. Ali's younger son, Hussein ibn Ali, led a rebellion against the Umayyads, but in 680 CE Hussein was defeated and killed at the battle of Karbala.

Nonetheless, the Umayyads faced further challenges. Despite the vast expansion of their empire, they continued to privilege Arabs and especially Syrians, treating non-Arab converts as second-class Muslims and barring them from official posts. They raised taxes to extreme levels, and were accused of impious behavior. Popular opposition to Umayyad rule grew steadily, centered on more zealous Muslims who wanted to return the caliphate to a descendant of the Prophet and who also offered to treat all Muslims, especially Persian converts, as equals. Raising a military force in Persia, the followers of Abu al-Abbas (who claimed descent from the Prophet through an uncle) defeated the Umayyads in 750 CE. Upon taking power, the new ruler shifted the capital from Damascus in Syria to Baghdad, where the Abbasid caliphs ruled for five hundred years, presiding over the fusion of Arabic and Persian culture that produced the Islamic Golden Age. A remnant of the Umayyads fled to Spain, where they established a rival caliphate in Cordoba.

The Abbasids' treatment of all Muslims who recognized the caliphate as equals was a social revolution, and persisted through the centuries up through the rule of the Ottoman Empire, which claimed the caliphate in the fifteenth century and moved it to Istanbul. All those who recognized the authority of the Abbasid and later Ottoman caliphate were known as Sunni Muslims. Yet a considerable fraction of Muslims did not recognize the Abbasid claim of descent from the Prophet and continued to look for a savior and future caliph from the line of Ali. They are known as Shi'a Muslims, and still commemorate Hussein's martyrdom at the battle of Karbala on the holiday of Ashura. In the sixteenth century the Safavid dynasty in Iran, seeking to justify its claims to power against its Ottoman rivals, adopted Shi'a as their official religion, producing a fusion of Iranian nationalism with the Shi'a faith. Conflict between Sunni and Shi'a Muslims continues to shape politics in the Middle East and North Africa to this day, influencing modern revolutionary movements in Bahrain, Iran, Iraq, Lebanon, Syria, and other nations.

Another early revolution with modern reverberations was the Maccabean Revolution in 164 BCE. After the death of Alexander the

Great, the Jewish lands of Palestine had come under the control of a Syrian dynasty, the Seleucids. The Seleucid rulers promoted the Greek religion and culture, which was attractive even to many Jews, so that the Jewish leadership grew divided between those accepting Greek customs and fundamentalists who urged strict adherence to traditional Jewish law. In 167 BCE the Seleucid King Antiochus IV sought to end Jewish practices and enforce Greek laws and worship; he outlawed temple sacrifices, circumcision, observance of the Sabbath and Jewish holidays, public readings of the Torah, and sought to establish worship of pagan gods in the Jewish temple. Some Jews, citing the might of Antiochus, went along with the changes. Others accepted execution rather than give up their traditional ways. But one group, led by the Jewish priest Mattathias and his sons in a village outside of Jerusalem, called themselves "Maccabees" (the hammer) and resolved to fight to restore Jewish worship and throw off Seleucid rule.

Their story reads like a modern revolution. The Maccabees began with guerrilla warfare against the Seleucid forces; building on early success they then raised a conventional army under the leadership of Mattathias's son Judah and his brothers. They developed a visionary ideology of opposition based on the book of Daniel and presented Judah as a modern version of the biblical Joshua who had liberated Canaan. Relying on superior zeal and tactics, they repeatedly defeated much larger military forces sent against them by the Seleucids; they also adroitly exploited divisions in the Seleucid leadership and benefitted from alliances with Sparta and Rome.

In 164 BCE, the Maccabees captured Jerusalem and celebrated by purifying the temple of all pagan cults and lighting the temple flame, which by legend burned for eight days on only a day's worth of oil. Fighting continued on and off for another twenty-three years until the last Syrian garrison was finally expelled. The Maccabees established a new Jewish dynasty in Palestine, imposed circumcision and other Jewish laws, and expanded their kingdom to include all of what is today modern Israel north of the Negev desert. To this day, Jews celebrate these events with the Festival of Lights, known as Chanukah, and the Maccabean Revolution inspires Jewish efforts to preserve an independent state of Israel. After several generations, though, Jewish independence was ended by the Romans, whose general Pompey invaded and took control of Israel in 63 BCE.

After the reign of Augustus, despite regional rebellions and civil wars among generals, and the division of the Roman Empire into Western (Latin) and Eastern (Greek) empires, there were no further revolutions for many centuries. The power of the Roman and Byzantine state, the quasi-divine status of the emperors, and the effectiveness of its legions prevailed against popular uprisings for more than a thousand years. Even after the Roman Empire in the West collapsed because of invasions by Frankish and Germanic tribes, when Charlemagne reestablished a large territorial empire in Europe spanning portions of France, Germany, and Italy, he claimed the mantle of Rome. In 800 CE he had himself crowned by the pope as Holy Roman Emperor, a title that his successors continued to claim up until the French Revolution.

When the German and French branches of Charlemagne's family empire separated, the German branch continued to claim the imperial title. Meanwhile, the kings of France and England also claimed divine right and indeed were thought to be endowed with certain divine powers, such as the ability to cure the skin disease of scrofula with the royal touch. Revolution as a mode of politics did not return to western Europe until the rise of new city-states in Italy in the Renaissance and the spread of religious skepticism during the Enlightenment.

Chapter 5
Revolutions of the Renaissance and Reformation

After the breakup of Charlemagne's empire, three major powers—the king of France, the German Holy Roman Emperor, and the pope (who had established a growing territory in Italy)—dominated Europe. In the cracks between these empires, along a line from central Italy up through southern and central Germany and into the Low countries, trading towns grew into commercial cities, with the strongest proclaiming themselves to be free city-states. The earliest and strongest of these arose in Northern Italy. In these cities, the growth of new commercial groups and their struggles with the older landed aristocracy over issues of religion and politics produced numerous revolutions.

Revolutions in Renaissance Italy

The Republic of Florence was founded in 1115, when the city rebelled against the Margrave of Tuscany. As the city grew richer, two major political factions developed: the Ghibellines who represented the landed aristocracy, and the Guelphs who were rich merchants and leaders of the major guilds. In 1250 the Guelphs drove the Ghibellines from power and forced the aristocrats to cut down their towers. Then in 1260, after a defeat by the neighboring city of Sienna, the Guelphs' rule was overturned and the Ghibellines returned to power. But this did not last either, as Ghibelline excesses stirred up popular uprisings, and papal intervention soon helped to restore the Guelphs.

In 1378 an uprising of the lower working classes led by the wool workers (the *ciompi*) overthrew the Guelphs. The workers stormed the prisons and state buildings, and declared a government by the people. The *ciompi* rule of Florence—perhaps the most democratic of this period—lasted almost three years before they were deposed by a party led by Salvestro de' Medici.

These class struggles faded in the early 1400s as the Medicis, who rose to wealth as bankers to the popes and gained immortal fame as magnificent patrons of Renaissance art, gradually took control of Florence. The Medicis dominated the Florentine Republic until 1494, when King Charles VIII of France invaded Italy. Piero de' Medici (known to history as "Piero the Unfortunate") humiliatingly capitulated to all of Charles's demands, and as a result was overthrown by Florence's most fanatical revolutionary leader, Girolamo Savonarola.

Savonarola was a Dominican friar and an early religious fundamentalist who wanted Florence to become a "city of God." He denounced clerical corruption and the exploitation of the poor. He ordered a "bonfire of the vanities," having ostentatious wigs, perfumes, paintings, and even ancient pagan manuscripts publicly burned. For four years Florence was ruled as a Christian commonwealth, with the Gospel as law, inspired by Savonarola's fiery preaching. Yet Savonarola went too far; his claims of prophecy brought him into conflict with the pope, who excommunicated him. As with many revolutionaries, people grew tired of living by extremes and turned on Savonarola. In 1498, his opponents took power and put Savonarola on trial for heresy and sedition. When his sentence was confirmed by the pope, the great preacher was hanged and burned in the public square.

2. Girolamo Savonarola being hanged and burned in Florence, 1498.

In the following decades, the Medicis returned to power in Florence and though briefly expelled by another popular revolt in 1527–30, eventually ended the Republic, becoming Dukes of Florence and later Grand Dukes of Tuscany.

Although Florence was the site of the most frequent and extreme revolutions of this period, throughout Italy parties associated with elite or populist groups contested for power. Advantage frequently shifted, with the winning party sometimes supported by the pope, sometimes by the emperor. In fact, our modern word for "revolutions" comes from this period, when Italians began to refer to the frequent rotations of power between different groups as a *revolutio*, from the Latin "revolvere," to cycle or revolve.

Revolutions in the Reformation

Savonarola was not the only monk repelled by corruption among the clergy. In Germany, Martin Luther, a monk and professor of theology, issued a fundamental challenge to the corruption and earthly power of the pope. The resulting Reformation swept Europe, giving rise to Lutheran and other reform groups, who often challenged Catholic rulers for political control. Followers of John Calvin of Geneva in particular sought to create governments that were "godly" in virtue rather than subservient to the evils of the papacy. In several cases—including the Dutch Revolt against Spain in the 1560s, and the English Revolution in the 1640s—Calvinists led political revolutions in the name of virtue.

The English Revolution was the first revolution in modern history to put a king on trial and formally execute him. In the late sixteenth and early seventeenth centuries, rapid population growth in England led to falling wages and a vast expansion of London. At the same time, rising prices and expenses led the Crown to sell lands and titles, creating an expanded and increasingly contentious elite. These elites, represented in Parliament, clashed with the king over matters of religion and taxation. By 1638 King Charles I had dismissed Parliament, expanded taxation by decree, imposed harsh and often arbitrary rule in Ireland, repressed English Calvinists (the Puritans), and, most foolishly, attempted to impose Anglican religious practices on Presbyterian Scotland. When the Scots raised an army to resist, Charles had to recall Parliament to ask for funds to respond.

From 1640 to 1642, Parliamentary leaders demanded ever greater concessions in return for granting funds. Yet Charles resisted any infringement on his powers. By the summer of 1642, as the power struggle intensified, Parliament had raised an army, drawing on the county militias and support from the City of London. To oppose them, Charles raised his standard at Nottingham in August and gathered an army of loyal royalists; the result was a series of civil wars.

Oliver Cromwell, a brilliant general known as "Old Ironsides," led the parliamentary forces to victory. Inspired by Puritan preachers, Cromwell and his army also sought to create a virtuous, godly state. After Charles was tried and executed in 1649, Cromwell became Lord Protector of the British Commonwealth. Under the Commonwealth, the House of Lords was abolished, as was the monarchy, and a Calvinist Church was established. In 1649 Parliament declared "that the people are, under God, the original of all just power; that the Commons of England, being chosen by and representing the people, have the supreme power in this nation."

But Cromwell too could not work with Parliament. Five months after his first Parliament met, Cromwell dissolved it and divided England into military districts, ruled by his chosen major-generals. After his death, people sought a return to normalcy, and in 1660 Charles's son was welcomed back to take the throne as Charles II. (Maybe not quite normalcy, for the Royalists did bear a grudge—they had Cromwell's body dug up from its grave in Westminster Abbey, hung in chains, and beheaded.)

The English Revolution and its aftermath inspired some of the most profound works of political theory in the English language, including John Milton's defense of free speech in *Areopagitica* (1644); Thomas Hobbes's argument for absolute sovereign authority, based on reason and the need to avoid civil violence, and one of the first works to study politics in terms of a social contract, in *Leviathan* (1651); and John Locke's defense of natural rights in *Two Treatises of Government* (1689).

Locke was one of the English leaders who contributed to what was perhaps the most significant revolution of this era, the "Glorious Revolution" of 1688–89. Britain had been a Protestant nation since Henry VIII's break with the papacy in the mid-1500s, with Anglicanism the official state religion and public Catholic worship illegal. Yet many Britons, including members of its royal family, remained adherents of the Roman Catholic faith. In 1685 Charles II died without children, and his Catholic brother became King James II. James sought to restore Catholic influence in Britain, reshaping the universities and appointing Catholics to leading positions in the government. Claiming divine right, he proclaimed that he had the right to dispense with any laws of Parliament he wished, and he dismissed Parliament. Concerned about the growing Puritan colonies in North America, he revoked their charters and remodeled all the colonies of New England, plus New York and New Jersey, into a single Dominion of New England under a royal governor.

After a male heir was born to James and his queen in 1688, a group of British Protestant leaders, fearing that they would be saddled with a Catholic succession, offered their support to William of Orange, the Protestant ruler of Holland, if he would bring an army to England to depose James. William had married James's daughter Mary, and he was promised that if successful they could rule England together. Later that year, William landed a large invasion force in southern England. Faced with these forces and defections from his own officers, James fled to France. Parliament ruled that James had thereby abdicated and offered William and Mary the throne as king and queen.

But the true significance of this revolution lay in the Toleration Act and the Bill of Rights, which Parliament passed in 1689. The Bill of Rights determined that Parliament would set the rules for succession to the throne, and set limits on the powers of the crown in domestic affairs including prohibiting taxation without Parliamentary consent, prohibiting the King from keeping a standing army without such consent, and granting the rights of Protestants to hold arms. The Bill also established the rights of Parliament, including freedom of speech in Parliament and the requirement to hold free and regular parliamentary elections, and gave rights to subjects, including duly impanelled juries and a ban on excessive bail and on cruel and unusual punishments. The

> ### From the English Bill of Rights (1689):
>
> "for the vindicating and asserting their ancient rights and liberties declare:
>
> - That the pretended power of suspending the laws or the execution of laws by regal authority without consent of Parliament is illegal;
> - That the pretended power of dispensing with laws or the execution of laws by regal authority, as it hath been assumed and exercised of late, is illegal;
> - That the commission for erecting the late Court of Commissioners for Ecclesiastical Causes, and all other commissions and courts of like nature, are illegal and pernicious;
> - That levying money for or to the use of the Crown by pretence of prerogative, without grant of Parliament, for longer time, or in other manner than the same is or shall be granted, is illegal;
> - That it is the right of the subjects to petition the king, and all commitments and prosecutions for such petitioning are illegal;
> - That the raising or keeping a standing army within the kingdom in time of peace, unless it be with consent of Parliament, is against law;

Toleration Act greatly expanded religious freedom. Although the act did not permit public worship by Catholics and allowed only Anglicans to hold state offices and university positions, it ended the discord between the Anglican Church and the other major Protestant groups. The act gave all Protestant sects that accepted the Holy Trinity the right to worship openly and without penalty. This enabled Baptists, Presbyterians, Quakers, and Independents to take prominent roles in England's economy and society.

It is hard to overstress the importance of these acts. For the first time since Augustus, the divine right of kings had been explicitly

- That the subjects which are Protestants may have arms for their defence suitable to their conditions and as allowed by law;
- That election of members of Parliament ought to be free;
- That the freedom of speech and debates or proceedings in Parliament ought not to be impeached or questioned in any court or place out of Parliament;
- That excessive bail ought not to be required, nor excessive fines imposed, nor cruel and unusual punishments inflicted;
- That jurors ought to be duly impanelled and returned, and jurors which pass upon men in trials for high treason ought to be freeholders;
- That all grants and promises of fines and forfeitures of particular persons before conviction are illegal and void;
- And that for redress of all grievances, and for the amending, strengthening and preserving of the laws, Parliaments ought to be held frequently.

And they do claim, demand and insist upon all and singular the premises as their undoubted rights and liberties . . ."

denied, with laws passed by Parliament clearly elevated over the will of the king, indeed with Parliament declaring its right to bestow the Crown. After several centuries in which the power of kings in Europe had been growing, with monarchs like Louis XVI in France, Frederick William I of Brandenburg-Prussia, and Philip IV of Spain diminishing their local parliaments and developing absolutist rule, the rights of Parliament in Britain were definitively upheld. And in sharp opposition to the practice established in the Treaty of Westphalia in 1648 and carried out with increasing vigor in most of Europe, where monarchs were entitled to choose a state religion and enforce its practice on their subjects, the Act of Toleration guaranteed freedom of worship for certain groups of dissenters from the established Anglican Church. Although the revolutionaries claimed that they were simply restoring the historical balance of power between the king and Parliament, these acts in fact embodied many of the ideas that would be at the core of the revolutions to come in America and France in the following century.

Chapter 6
Constitutional revolutions: America, France, Europe (1830 and 1848), and Meiji Japan

From ancient times up through the seventeenth century, revolutionaries thought of themselves as fighting for justice and creating new regimes, but they did so in traditional terms. That is, they might overthrow their king, or fight for a government that supported one religion against another, or even create a free republic and reject the authority of local kings or dukes. Yet they never fought against kingship as such or religion itself as unjust institutions. They always relied on some form of state-supported religion and some kind of traditional authority to maintain order.

The most radical revolutions of the ancient world, those that created the city-states and constitutions of Athens, Sparta, Rome, and other republics, built on local custom and religion. The leader of England's Puritan Revolution, Oliver Cromwell, who saw the execution of the king and the creation of a Commonwealth, nonetheless spoke in 1654 to defend "the ranks and orders of men,—whereby England hath been known for hundreds of years. . . . A nobleman, a gentleman, a yeoman; the distinction of these: that is a good interest of the nation, and a great one!" And the revolutionaries of 1688, who created what we now in retrospect call a constitutional monarchy—that is, a monarch bound by the laws of an elected parliament—had no idea or plan to create a constitution. Rather, they believed they were simply restoring the traditional balance in England between Crown and Parliament, ruling jointly, and they called their revolution "Glorious" because they believed it reestablished a golden order of the past.

The idea that a revolution is a fundamental break with the past, that revolutionaries can create something entirely new by force of will and frame a government using the principles of reason—not custom or religion—is something distinctly modern.

In the course of the seventeenth and eighteenth centuries, as scientific discoveries caused people to become skeptical about the truth of religious authority, and to put more faith in reason and practical experience, ideas about governance changed as well, with revolutionary implications. People began to doubt that rulers had a divine right to rule and instead started to see monarchy as simply an old custom that need not bind modern men. They also began to see churches as institutions that people created to choose their own ways to worship God, not divine institutions to which people owed complete obedience. This growing skepticism and secularism led to a modern twist in revolutions—revolutionaries that attacked the rights of kings and the rights of churches as such and who drew up constitutions, based on reason and the concept of natural rights, to liberate men (though not yet women) from these authorities.

The American Revolution

The British colonies of North America were founded in the early 1600s by commercial companies and religious groups seeking freedom from British society: Puritans in New England, Quakers in Pennsylvania, Catholics in Maryland, and plantation colonies in Virginia. Yet all the colonies obtained charters from the British Crown, and although they elected their own local legislatures, they were still ruled by British governors as subjects of the Crown. The colonies grew rapidly and prospered by trading tobacco, wheat, cotton, timber, and furs. As they pushed west into the Appalachians, British government forces played a key role in defeating the French and their Native American allies in the French and Indian War (1754–1763), which secured the colonies' claims over all land east of the Mississippi.

The war was expensive, and the British government was determined to recover its costs from the colonists by imposing new taxes on colonial trade and consumption. When the colonists refused to pay these new taxes (including a demonstration in which chests of British tea were dumped into Boston Harbor), sharp divisions arose between rebels and loyalists. While the latter supported British rule, many colonial elites, from Virginia plantation owners to New York and Boston bankers and lawyers, as well as popular groups, were outraged that they were being forced to pay for Britain's wars without any say or consent.

The American colonists believed they enjoyed the rights that Englishmen had won in the Revolution of 1688–89, to have a Parliament of their choosing agree to any taxes and to rule together with the king. By the 1770s many felt they were being ruled despotically by a faraway king and that their basic liberties were being stripped away. American orators made stirring speeches about rights and liberties. Perhaps the most famous was Patrick Henry's bold plea, as he persuaded his fellow Virginians to join the revolutionary cause: "Is life so dear, or peace so sweet, as to be purchased at the price of chains and slavery? . . . Give me Liberty or give me Death!"

Thomas Paine's pamphlet *Common Sense*, published in January 1776, argued that it was absurd for an island like Britain to claim to rule a continent like America; that all men were created equal and owed no allegiance to a distant king who had no interest in the welfare of Americans; and that America should hold a continental congress and draw up a charter of independence. In July, American leaders did just that, publishing the *Declaration of Independence*, drafted by Thomas Jefferson. The *Declaration* stated that King George III was an unjust king who had violated

Americans' "self-evident . . . rights [to] Life, Liberty, and the pursuit of Happiness," and that the purpose of government was to secure these rights, "deriving their just powers from the consent of the governed."

This extraordinary claim—that the power of kings came not from God but that all governments should derive their power from consent of the governed—led to eight years of war with Britain, which sought to enforce its claims to royal rule. George Washington, the colonists' general, brilliantly organized and shepherded the ragged colonial army through several years when mere survival was remarkable. Eventually, France decided that it could avenge its defeat in the French and Indian War by helping the colonies against Britain, providing first financial support and then military intervention.

In late 1781, American and French armies, supported by a French fleet, besieged the British Army at Yorktown, Virginia. Completely surrounded and cut off from reinforcements, the British General Cornwallis surrendered. Washington and his allies captured seven thousand British troops. These losses proved decisive; six months later the British Parliament voted to stop the war, and the American colonies had gained their independence.

The thirteen colonies had begun adopting new state constitutions in the late 1770s. These constitutions were among the most democratic ever seen. They broke sharply with European traditions by outlawing any distinctions of rank and title. Many had bills of rights to protect citizens from state authority and gave the vote to a wide range of male citizens (New Jersey even briefly gave women the vote but withdrew their suffrage in 1807). Relations among the states were regulated by the Articles of Confederation, which were ratified in 1781.

Yet the Articles almost immediately were seen to be inadequate. There were no rules to regulate trade or create a common currency among the states, and the central government was too weak to aid the states with their debts or manage national defense. So in 1787 a national convention met in Philadelphia to draft a new federal constitution.

Since most loyalists had fled to Canada, the new government faced no major internal counterrevolutionary threats, and once British forces withdrew, America was also secure from foreign invasion. Under these favorable conditions, the idea of a stronger central government was controversial. Debates dragged on and many compromises were made, including retention of slavery. But in a masterpiece of political argument, now known as the *Federalist Papers*, James Madison, John Jay, and Alexander Hamilton defended the new constitution. Harking back to the Roman revolution against its foreign kings, signing their papers "Publius," they successfully argued that America should become a representative republic, with a Senate, House of Representatives, and president, all directly or indirectly chosen by the vote of qualified citizens. The new constitution was ratified in 1788, and

3. The signing of the United States Constitution, 1787.

later that year George Washington was elected the first president of the United States of America.

The French Revolution

The American Revolution seemed radical to Europeans, but it was also quite distant. Yet revolution would soon strike the largest country in Europe. Despite France's success in the American War of Independence, its accumulated war debts and the imminent expiration of wartime tax measures created a fiscal crisis. When French law courts and notables rejected proposed new taxes, the king was pressured to call a meeting of the representatives of the three estates of the realm—the clergy, nobility, and commoners—to seek a solution.

The Estates met in May 1789, after a year of famine had spurred riots across the country, and expectations ran high for major political and economic reforms. Yet the Estates immediately broke down into acrimony. The clergy and nobility insisted on voting by Estates, so that their votes would always outweigh those of the commoners, known as the Third Estate. However, this Third Estate was filled with professionals and bureaucrats who had sought or were even in the process of acquiring noble status themselves, since the eighteenth century had been a period of considerable social mobility; they were enraged at being treated as insignificant. Their rage was shared by abbots and priests who were also treated as commoners by the privileged bishops. The Abbé Sieyès wrote: "What is the Third Estate? Everything. What has it been until now in the public order? Nothing."

After weeks of deadlock, the representatives of the Third Estate proclaimed that they spoke for the entire nation. Reconstituting themselves as the National Assembly and joined by reformers from the other Estates, they set out to reshape France. They produced a Declaration of the Rights of Man and of the Citizen, and from 1789 to 1793 the Assembly, and the elected Legislative Assembly and

National Convention that followed, abolished the monarchy and all feudal privileges, executed the king and queen, and nationalized the Catholic Church and sold off its lands. Following the American example, they declared France to be a republic, under the motto *Liberté, Égalité, Fraternité*. The French revolutionaries saw themselves as repeating the feats of the early Romans who had overthrown their king, depicting French leaders in togas and calling their military leaders "consuls" after the old Roman term.

The actions of the national assemblies and conventions were spurred by popular uprisings in Paris and the provinces. In 1789, fearing that the king would disperse the new National Assembly, Parisian workers armed themselves and attacked a royal fortress, the Bastille. Supported by a detachment of renegade soldiers with artillery, the crowds took the Bastille on July 14.

Foreign powers grew alarmed and attacked the new republic. Within France, several provinces resisted the nationalization of

4. The storming of the Bastille, July 14, 1789.

the church and the new demands of the revolutionary government, producing a civil war as well. Under these strains, radicals formed a Committee of Public Safety. Maximilian Robespierre and his colleagues on the committee led a reign of terror, executing accused enemies of the revolution in Paris and the provinces by the thousands. Robespierre even had several fellow revolutionaries guillotined, but eventually he too was brought to meet Madame Guillotine, and the radicals were deposed and replaced by a more moderate and pragmatic government.

French armies then spread across Europe, fomenting republican revolutions near and far. After 1801, the French Revolution came under the control of the wildly popular and successful general Napoleon Bonaparte. Napoleon advanced himself from consul to emperor, and like the ancient Romans, commissioned triumphal arches (the Arc de Triomphe) to mark his conquests. The Vendôme Column in Paris, modeled after Trajan's column in Rome, bears a statue of Napoleon wearing a toga and crowned with a laurel wreath.

Napoleon's string of victories ended on the outskirts of Moscow, where he was turned back by the Russian winter and the stubborn resistance of Russian forces. After Napoleon was defeated by a coalition of European powers in 1814, he was exiled and the Bourbon kings were restored to the French throne.

By then the belief that government belonged in the hands of citizens, not kings, had become widespread. The French Revolution—with its popular attacks on aristocrats, revolutionary terror, creation of a new constitutional order, and military success and expansion under Napoleon—soon became the prototype of a revolution for succeeding generations.

Even in France's sugar colony of Saint Domingue in Haiti, slaves and former slaves followed the proclamation that all men were equal and citizens, and rose up to demand their freedom from the plantation owners and from France. After years of struggle, led by Toussaint Louverture, a former slave turned prosperous plantation owner, Haiti won its freedom.

The European revolutions of 1830 and 1848

In 1830 revolution broke out again in France, and also in Belgium and Switzerland. In France and Belgium, the revolutionaries succeeded in forcing a change of ruler and the acceptance of constitutional monarchies, modeled on Great Britain. Although the Belgian monarchy exists to this day, in France it lasted only eighteen years. In 1848 an even larger wave of constitutional revolutions swept Europe. These revolutions produced a republic in France, a constitutional monarchy in Denmark, a new federal constitution in Switzerland, and briefly drove absolute monarchs from power in Prussia, the states of southern and western Germany, Austria, Sicily, Lombardy, Hungary, and Romania.

These constitutional revolutions were led by professionals and students pursuing the ideals of the French and American Revolutions and pushed forward by peasant revolts and urban uprisings, the latter occurring in the wake of sustained population growth and spikes in food prices in 1847–48. Yet the elite constitutional leaders never made common cause with the popular groups. No broad cross-class coalition arose to overcome the aristocratic and military elites, who remained loyal to the monarchies. In 1849 Russian troops backed counterrevolutionary actions by the forces of the Austrian Empire and Prussia, reversing most of the gains outside of France and Denmark. The success of this counterrevolutionary thrust has led most historians to label the events of 1848 as a failed or abortive revolution. Even in France, the republic was short-lived. Louis Bonaparte, Napoleon's nephew, trading on his famous name, was elected as the first president of France in 1848. A few years later, like his more famous uncle, he staged a coup against the republic and named himself Emperor Napoleon III.

From 1849 to 1871 conservatism reigned in Europe, and it appeared that the clock was turning back toward monarchies. Yet this was not to be. In 1871, after Prussia defeated Napoleon III in the Franco-Prussian War, the residents of Paris proclaimed the city to be a revolutionary commune, freed from the erstwhile emperor. Although the revolutionaries were eventually suppressed by a national French Army, the army itself made no attempt to restore the empire. Instead, it proclaimed the Third French Republic; France has been a republic ever since.

The ideas of democracy and constitutional government continued to spread; the Italian states were united as a constitutional monarchy in 1861, and even the Prussian minister Bismarck began granting constitutional rights to Germany's peoples. In 1918, following Germany's defeat in World War I, a worker's revolution helped topple the last German monarch and install the Weimar Republic. By the end of World War I, every state in Europe had thrown off their absolute monarchies, and all but Russia had become parliamentary, constitutional regimes.

Meiji Japan

Constitutional government became widely sought-after outside of Europe as well. Identifying constitutional government with the military, technological, and economic success of the European powers, reformers around the world wanted to replace their empires and monarchies with constitutional regimes.

Japan had been ruled since the early seventeenth century by the Tokugawa Shoguns. These military rulers, based in the capital of Edo (Tokyo), were supported by aristocratic governors *(daimyo)* and a privileged class of warriors *(samurai)* who lorded over the common peasants and artisans. Yet in the nineteenth century, the Shoguns had been financially weakened by growing debts to the rice merchants of Osaka, while several of the *daimyos* had started to modernize their own military forces and administrations with western ideas and technology. In 1852, the U.S. Navy Commodore Matthew Perry sailed a fleet of modern steam-powered warships into Tokyo Bay in an impressive display of force. Sweeping aside all resistance, he imposed a humiliating treaty on the Shogun.

Having determined that the Shogun's regime was outmoded and incapable of defending Japan, modernizing leaders from two southern provinces undertook a revolutionary war to overthrow it. Proclaiming their loyalty to the Japanese emperor—who had been a ceremonial figurehead under the Shoguns—the leaders of this so-called Meiji Restoration claimed only to be restoring the primacy of the emperor. After they defeated the Shogun and took power in 1868, ending more than six centuries of Shogun rule, they revolutionized Japanese society and politics. The Meiji leaders abolished the rank and privileges of the samurai, created a legislative assembly (the Diet), and eventually produced a new constitution.

Rapidly adopting western modes of education, military organization, and technology, yet retaining their own distinct Japanese national culture and unity, the Meiji regime presided over rapid industrialization and the development of a modern army and navy. In 1905 Japan defeated the once-feared Russian military, helping undermine the legitimacy of the Russian government and contributing to the soon-to-follow Russian Revolution.

The Meiji regime in turn became a direct source of constitutional change in China, as many of the leaders of the Chinese Republican Revolution of 1911 had studied in Japan. Sun Yat-sen, the leader of the revolution, organized the republican opposition from Tokyo.

Despite their uneven successes, the constitutional revolutions created a new template for revolution. Henceforth, "revolution" would not mean the mere overthrow of a tyrant but the destruction

Thomas Paine on the worthlessness of kings:

In England a king hath little more to do than to make war and give away places; which, in plain terms, is to impoverish the nation and set it together by the ears. A pretty business indeed for a man to be allowed eight hundred thousand sterling a year for, and worshipped into the bargain! Of more worth is one honest man to society, and in the sight of God, than all the crowned ruffians that ever lived.

—*Common Sense* (1776)

Thomas Jefferson on natural rights:

We hold these truths to be self-evident, that all men are created equal, that they are endowed by their Creator with certain unalienable Rights, that among these are Life, Liberty and the pursuit of Happiness.—That to secure these rights, Governments are instituted among Men, deriving their just powers from the consent of the governed,—That whenever any Form of Government becomes destructive of these ends, it is the Right of the People to alter or to abolish it, and to institute new Government, laying its foundation on such principles and organizing its powers in such form, as to them shall seem most likely to effect their Safety and Happiness.

—*The Declaration of Independence* (1776)

The Meiji Constitution of 1889 on the rights of Japanese subjects, creating a constitutional monarchy under the emperor of Japan:

Article 23. No Japanese subject shall be arrested, detained, tried or punished, unless according to law.

Article 24. No Japanese subject shall be deprived of his right of being tried by the judges determined by law.

Article 25. Except in the cases provided for in the law, the house of no Japanese subject shall be entered or searched without his consent.

Article 26. Except in the cases mentioned in the law, the secrecy of the letters of every Japanese subject shall remain inviolate.

Article 27. The right of property of every Japanese subject shall remain inviolate.

(2) Measures necessary to be taken for the public benefit shall be any provided for by law.

Article 28. Japanese subjects shall, within limits not prejudicial to peace and order, and not antagonistic to their duties as subjects, enjoy freedom of religious belief.

Article 29. Japanese subjects shall, within the limits of law, enjoy the liberty of speech, writing, publication, public meetings and associations.

of traditional regimes and their replacement by new, constitutional governments based on universal rights and the consent of the governed. From its origins in America and France, this model has spread to become the dominant ideal of revolution today.

Yet for much of the twentieth century, this ideal was supplanted by another model: that of communist revolution.

Chapter 7
Communist revolutions: Russia, China, and Cuba

Karl Marx, a German philosopher and journalist, along with his friend the industrialist Frederick Engels, observed that in early nineteenth-century Britain the conditions of industrial workers were appalling. Child labor, twelve- and even sixteen-hour workdays, and repetitive work with the new machines seemed to them inhuman. They concluded that although the revolutions of the eighteenth and early nineteenth centuries had overturned kings and brought constitutions, the benefits seemed to go entirely to the new capitalist class of bankers, merchants, and manufacturers. Marx developed a theory of history that argued for progress through a series of class revolutions: First the capitalists would throw out the absolute kings and hereditary nobles; then it was equally inevitable that the workers would rise up and throw out the capitalists. Marx predicted a global surge of workers' revolutions against the capitalists and the liberal constitutional states. They would be replaced with communist states in which all property was owned by society as a whole, not used to exploit the great mass of workers for the benefit of a small capitalist elite.

Marx was only partially right. In Europe and North America, workers did band together but not for revolution. Rather, they formed unions and backed labor and workers' parties, which raised their wages, limited hours, and provided gradually increasing social benefits. Meanwhile, in the still early industrializing and agrarian states of Russia and China, intellectuals dreamed of making a grand leap from peasant societies all the way to communist states. It was therefore in the still mainly agrarian states outside of Europe that Marx's wave of communist revolutions occurred.

The Russian Revolution

In the nineteenth century, Russia was the largest but most backward state in Europe. Its peasants remained serfs until 1861, and even when liberated were saddled with heavy redemption payments to their landlords. Industrial centers were few, mainly concentrated in the iron- and copper-producing regions of the Ural Mountains and the factory districts of Saint Petersburg and Moscow. The tsar ruled absolutely through his aristocratic officials and military.

In 1905, following Russia's defeat by Japan, peasant rebellions broke out in the countryside, massive strikes spread through Moscow and Saint Petersburg, and sailors mutinied in several ports. Although the disorders were put down by the army, the regime took fright and accelerated its efforts at political and economic reform. An advisory elected parliament (the Duma) was created and land reforms were begun. But radical thinkers wanted even greater changes. Vladimir Lenin developed the idea of a vanguard communist party, which would lead the workers and carry the peasantry with them, sweeping away the tsar and his nobles and creating a communist society.

The progress of reforms was interrupted by the outbreak of World War I. During this crucial period, even aristocrats were distressed that the weak-minded Tsar Nicholas II and Empress Alexandra were distracted by a wild Russian mystic and healer, Grigori Rasputin. Though Rasputin was eventually killed (a difficult task, for he was poisoned, shot, *and* drowned) his influence undermined popular and elite respect for the court.

Germany inflicted major defeats and huge losses on Russia's army in 1914–16, provoking Russian elites to seek greater control over policy and the populace to protest against the war. On International Women's day, February 23, 1917, thousands of women demonstrated against bread shortages in the capital. In the following week, hundreds of thousands of workers and students joined the protests. When soldiers fired on the crowds, other military units defected and joined the insurgents, who attacked police stations and tsarist officials. The Duma persuaded the court that only the tsar's abdication would restore order, and then established a provisional government. On March 3, the tsar abdicated, ending the reign of the Romanovs.

Yet the provisional government's efforts to continue the war provoked the anger of the industrial workers of Moscow and Saint Petersburg and of peasants throughout the country. Workers organized themselves into councils (called soviets) and were recruited by the communists. Soldiers and sailors began to defect. A few months later, in October 1917, Lenin's vanguard communist party, the Bolsheviks, was able to stage a bloodless coup, organizing its supporters to silently take over the post offices, railroads, and government buildings of the capital in the dead of night. On October 25th, Russia awoke to find itself with a new communist government.

But taking control of the entire country would not be so easy. Tsarist generals raised a counterrevolutionary, anticommunist White Army to take back the country from the "reds." Lenin's communists, with the organizational genius of Leon Trotsky, created a Red Army from defecting soldiers, supportive workers, and drafted peasants. Civil war raged from 1918 to 1921, fought with ruthless brutality on both sides. To prevent the tsar's family from becoming a rallying point, they were all executed, even the children. Compelling experienced officers to fight for them, using central position and control of the rail lines through Moscow, and drawing on the greater support of workers and peasants for the communists, the Red Army triumphed.

5. A White Army poster depicting Leon Trotsky as the deadly Red Menace of the Russian Revolution, sitting on the wall of the Kremlin, 1919.

During the civil war, Lenin enforced "war communism" in which the party took total control of the economy and claimed all assets. After the war, in order to speed recovery from the devastation, Lenin followed a so-called New Economic Policy (NEP), which allowed peasants and small private businesses to take their products to market. But after Lenin's death in 1924, a struggle for leadership arose between those who wanted to continue with the NEP, and those who sought to restore full communist control of all sectors of the economy. The latter faction, led by Joseph Stalin, won this battle, and Stalin became the new leader of the Communist Party.

In the 1930s, Stalin carried out a ruthless program of collectivization of all peasant farms, draining food from the countryside to invest in a crash industrialization program. Millions of peasants perished as Stalin's forces scoured the countryside for stores of grain and directed as much as possible to workers in the cities. When faced with opposition to his policies, Stalin unleashed a terror campaign of purges, show trials, and executions of his enemies, creating a vast "gulag" of prisons all across the Soviet Union. Even Trotsky had to flee, only to be assassinated while overseas.

Stalin's efforts to create a modern industrial base helped the Soviet Union defeat Nazi Germany during World War II and to become a global superpower after the war, when the Soviets created and supported communist regimes all across Eastern Europe. Nonetheless, the Soviet Union itself would fall to revolution before the end of the century.

China's Communist Revolution

Mao Zedong, the leader of China's Communist Revolution, was born in 1893, at the twilight of China's Imperial era. The son of a peasant grain merchant, Mao placed the peasantry at the core of his communist revolution. Mao made many mistakes; tragically, his policies killed tens of millions. Nonetheless, he restored China's independence after a century of defeats and humiliations by foreign powers, and his Communist Party raised China to become the world's second largest economy.

In the mid-seventeenth century, Manchu invaders from the north had entered China and established the Qing dynasty. Under Qing rule, China became the richest country in the world, widely admired even in Europe. Yet by the nineteenth century, Western progress in technology and arms had left China far behind. In the 1840s, European powers and the United States began to take control of China's overseas trade, imposing highly unequal treaties. As the Qing emperor's grip was weakened by foreign intervention, and the empire's administration was strained by rapid population growth, anti-Manchu sentiment and disorders began to spread. In the 1850s, the great Taiping Rebellion devastated southern China, killing millions. In 1900, seven years after Mao's birth, an antiforeigner movement known as the Boxers attacked Europeans living in Beijing. In reaction, American and European forces occupied the capital and demanded huge indemnities from the Chinese government.

As its power waned, the Qing dynasty tried to reform and modernize China's armed forces, schools, and officials. At the same time, revolutionary organizations arose aiming to replace imperial rule with a constitutional government. These organizations drew support from officials, businessmen, professionals, students, workers and overseas Chinese, all seeking to expel the Manchu rulers and strengthen China. From 1907 to 1911, in what is known as the Chinese Republican Revolution, anti-Manchu uprisings broke out in many cities and provinces. In late 1911, units of the New Army—which had been created by recent Qing reforms— defected and joined the rebels to seize control of several major cities. (The teenage Mao Zedong briefly joined one of the rebel armies.) The provisional government of the Republic of China was created in January 1912; the next month the Qing emperor abdicated, ending more than two thousand years of Imperial rule. Sun Yat-sen, a physician and intellectual who had been an early anti-Manchu revolutionary leader, became its first president.

The new republic did not last long, for new power struggles soon emerged. In 1912, Yuan Shikai, an ambitious general under the late Qing, took over as president. Forcing Sun to flee to Japan, Yuan appointed generals to rule the provinces. In 1915 he attempted, unsuccessfully, to restore the monarchy with himself as emperor. When Yuan died in 1916, China dissolved into warlord rule.

The following year, Sun Yat-sen returned from Japan, determined to restore the republic. By 1921, he had established a military government in southern China, led by his Chinese Nationalist Party (in Chinese, the Guomindang, or GMD). When Sun died in 1925, Chiang Kai-shek, a general who had fought for Sun, became the new Nationalist Party leader.

Meanwhile, Mao returned to school. After graduating from college in 1918, he moved to Beijing and joined a group of scholars who, following the communist revolution in Russia, were drawn to Marxism-Leninism. Mao became an early leader of the Chinese Communist Party (CCP), founded in 1921. Still, it would take almost three decades of organizing and civil war before Mao would come to power.

From 1922 to 1927, the CCP worked with the GMD, helping the latter to gain Soviet support. In 1926–27, the Communists and Nationalists cooperated in a major military offensive, known as the Northern Expedition, directed against the warlords. But in 1927 Chiang viciously turned on his erstwhile allies and began a "White terror" campaign to wipe out the communists. Thousands were massacred in Shanghai that April, and in the following years hundreds of thousands of communists, communist sympathizers, suspected communists, and others were hunted down and killed across the country.

Mao then argued that the CCP should take advantage of the peasant uprisings that had occurred during the Northern Expedition and raise a peasant army. He was opposed by other CCP leaders, who followed the orthodox view that only an industrial proletariat could be the core of a communist party.

Eventually, Mao's strategy was proved correct. Forced to retreat far inland to evade Chiang's forces, in 1930 Mao established a rural base in Jiangxi in southern China. Carrying out land reforms and building up his peasant Red Army, Mao gained control of an area that he proclaimed the "Soviet Republic of China." The following year Japan invaded Manchuria, forcing the GMD to turn its attention to defending China against the Japanese. Nonetheless, Chiang remained determined to wipe out Mao's forces.

In 1934 Chiang's Nationalist army succeeded in surrounding Mao's Soviet. Breaking through the Nationalist lines, eighty thousand communists set out on a Long March to reach another communist base in distant Shaanxi in northern China. Fighting constantly and traversing more than six thousand miles of rugged terrain over the course of a full year, only about eight thousand arrived at their destination. But the trials of the Long March toughened the CCP leadership, who became legendary for their endurance.

Meanwhile, Japan was planning to push deeper into China. In 1937 Japanese forces carried out a full invasion, taking Beijing, Shanghai, and Nanjing. In order to win more support, the communists turned to fight the Japanese. Building up their forces to several hundred thousand, from 1937 to 1945 they entered into a patriotic alliance with the GMD against Japan. Yet the differences between the GMD and CCP were becoming increasingly clear. The GMD remained based in the cities, and its leaders grew increasingly corrupt, benefiting from generous aid from the United States. The CCP built its base in peasant communities in the countryside; its leaders were known to be less corrupt, more efficient, and more concerned with the welfare of the population in the territories it controlled.

When the Americans defeated the Japanese in 1945, civil war resumed between the GMD and CCP. The CCP, with extensive help from the Soviet Union, built up a large conventional army. Meanwhile, the corruption of the Nationalists sapped the morale and effectiveness of its forces. The Nationalist government printed money with abandon, creating a galloping inflation; it also treated the populations of areas it liberated from the Japanese as traitors, imposing heavy requisitions and tolerating profiteering by regime cronies. Mao's forces swept the GMD out of more and more areas. Finally in October 1949, Mao entered Beijing and proclaimed the People's Republic of China. Chiang and the remaining Nationalist forces fled to Taiwan.

Once in power the communists pursued revolution relentlessly. Following the Soviet model, they nationalized all farmland and organized the population into collectives. They also sought to build up an industrial base, following the Stalinist emphasis on heavy industry. Then in the Great Leap Forward of 1958–60 Mao broke with the Soviet Union to forge his own pathway to economic development. Where the Soviet Union had focused on creating an industrial factory workforce, constructing massive iron and steel works and new manufacturing centers, Mao placed his focus on the peasantry. Dreaming of a rural, peasant-led economic growth surge, Mao encouraged peasants to form communes, which would strive for vast increases in the output of iron, steel, and machinery through local "backyard furnaces." But Mao's dream soon became a nightmare. His strategy produced chaos, as poorly built machines fell apart and peasants melted down their farm tools to meet targets for producing iron. Neglecting the harvest and giving up their farm tools caused a catastrophic shortage in food production. While propaganda posters showed well-fed peasants bringing in bumper harvests, people were reduced to eating grass, tree bark, and insects; tens of millions starved to death. By 1960, Mao turned over economic planning to his more pragmatic colleagues Zhou Enlai, Liu Shaoqi, and Deng Xiaoping.

Matters improved in the early 1960s, but by 1966 Mao became convinced that China was becoming too materialistic and had forgotten its revolutionary ideals. Mao therefore launched a campaign promoting "continuous revolution." His "Little Red Book" of revolutionary slogans, *Quotations from Chairman Mao*, was published by the army and became one of the most printed books in history, helping to create a personality cult around Mao and his ideas. In this "Great Proletarian Cultural Revolution," schools were closed and tens of millions of youth became Red Guards, encouraged by Mao to attack CCP officials, intellectuals, factory managers, and professionals. Mao turned on his rivals in the CCP, driving them from power. Millions of

6. Chinese revolutionary propaganda poster, showing a bountiful harvest during the famine of the Great Leap Forward, 1958.

university students and skilled professionals, including Deng Xiaoping, were exiled into rural villages to do manual labor.

After a few years, with schools and factories no longer functioning and armed conflict between rival factions threatening to plunge the country into civil war, the army stepped in to restore order. However, power struggles continued between the radical Gang of Four, led by Mao's wife, and more pragmatic party leaders. In 1976 both Zhou Enlai and Mao died, and the Gang of Four were arrested, ending the second radical phase of the revolution. By 1978 Deng had emerged as the new leader of the Communist Party.

The pragmatic Deng launched a campaign to completely restructure China's economy. A one-child family program was implemented to restrain China's runaway population growth. Communes were broken up and land was leased to peasants, who were permitted to sell their surplus output. Towns and communes were encouraged to start enterprises and were permitted to buy and sell at market prices. Special enclaves were created to court foreign investment and produce goods for export, a practice so successful it spread to the entire country. The government made huge investments in infrastructure, housing, energy, and other construction, and encouraged stock sales and privatization of state-owned enterprises.

Today, the CCP remains in command, but China is no longer a communist society. China has become the world's second largest economy, with international companies, a large profit-seeking business class, and workers and farmers aggressively seeking better conditions. Party leaders talk of an eventual transition to democracy, but Deng harshly repressed pro-democracy demonstrations in Tiananmen Square in 1989, and current party leaders show no sign of loosening their grip on power. Still, as the economy slows and resentment against the corruption of CCP officials spreads, one has to wonder if there will be yet another phase of revolution in China's future.

The Cuban Revolution

While the death tolls in the tens of millions under communist rule were kept hidden for decades, the rapid economic growth and growing military power of Russia and China were enormously attractive to aspiring leaders of developing countries. Communism became the preferred ideology of many champions of the poor, as well as those seeking to free their countries from domination by western capitalist countries, whether they were colonies of western nations or simply ruled by dictators with close ties to the West.

In the 1950s, Fidel Castro raised a peasant guerrilla army and drew on support from sugar workers to overthrow the Cuban dictatorship of Fulgencio Batista and establish a communist regime. Batista had created a classic personalist government in Cuba. In 1952 he cancelled scheduled elections and used the army to take over the country, relying on the support of elites connected to foreign business investments. Sugar constituted 80 percent of Cuba's exports, and almost half of sugar production was by U.S.-owned firms. American businesses also had extensive holdings in tourism, hotels, gambling, utilities, manufacturing, mining, and oil refining. The United States had helped Cuba win independence from Spain in the 1890s but then had repeatedly interfered in its politics to protect U.S. businesses. By the 1950s, many Cubans saw the Batista regime as little more than a front for U.S. interests. While Cuba was more prosperous than most Latin American countries (its life expectancy was fifth highest), peasants and workers in sugar refineries and other industries resented the wealth and corruption of those linked to foreign interests and the Batista regime.

One major center of opposition was the University of Havana. A brilliant young law graduate, Fidel Castro, had planned to run for Congress in the 1952 elections. But when these were cancelled, he began to hatch plans for an armed insurrection to unseat Batista. Castro's revolutionary campaign was remarkable for his miraculous escapes and good luck overcoming repeated failures.

On July 26, 1953, Fidel Castro, his brother Raul, and just over one hundred companions attacked the Moncada military barracks in Santiago, on the far eastern end of Cuba. The attack was a fiasco— almost half the rebels were killed and the rest captured. At their trial, Fidel gave a stirring speech against Batista, claiming that "history will absolve me." Nonetheless, the rebels were sentenced to fifteen years in a maximum security prison. A year and a half later they were freed, as Batista sought to improve his public image by granting an amnesty to the Moncada rebels.

The Castro brothers fled to Mexico to plan their next step. There they met Che Guevara, an Argentine physician who had traveled around Latin America. Che had become a radical advocate for the poor and had been outraged by the American overthrow of a populist government in Guatemala. Joining the Castros, Che and seventy-nine other Cuban exiles sailed an old and overloaded yacht, the *Granma*, to Cuba, landing there on December 2, 1956. Shortly after docking, they fell into an ambush by Cuban military forces. Only the Castros, Che, and about a dozen of their supporters survived. This little band fled into the Sierra Maestre in eastern Cuba. There they recruited peasants with promises of eventual land reform, schooling, and health care and trained them as guerrilla fighters.

That might have been the end, but the Castros were skillful; using hit-and-run tactics they managed to evade and outfight the forces that Batista sent after them, and their ranks swelled. Meanwhile, urban revolts and strikes by other opponents of the regime were harshly repressed, leaving the Castros' forces as the only open resistance to the regime. As Castro's prestige and reputation grew, Batista became more aggressive; in 1957 and early 1958 his forces tortured and executed hundreds of middle-class youth and workers who had joined in actions against him. In March 1958, revolted by Batista's violence and seeing Castro as a moderate nationalist leader, U.S. President Dwight Eisenhower halted arms shipments to Batista.

7. Leaders of the Cuban Revolution in a rare snapshot: Vilma Espin, Fidel Castro, Raul Castro, and Celia Sanchez, 1957.

After the arms embargo, morale in Batista's forces rapidly declined. In late 1958, Castro sent several hundred rebels out of the mountains toward the cities in the east. Batista's army refused to fight them, and Castro's forces took the cities of Santa Clara and Santiago unhindered. On January 1, 1959, Batista fled, and a few weeks later Castro entered Havana with enormous popular support.

After taking power, Castro nationalized foreign business operations and undertook land reforms. True to his word, he began national literacy and health campaigns, building thousands of new schools and clinics. Castro believed that only a communist-style revolution could bring justice to Cuba, given its long domination by foreign business interests. Yet for nearly two years Castro did not openly proclaim his intention to establish a communist state, fearing the United States would move to crush his revolution. After John F. Kennedy became president, furious Cuban business elites who had fled from the revolution convinced the American

CIA to finance an invasion by Cuban refugees and exiles, which would overthrow Castro and restore democracy. The invasion took place at the Bay of Pigs on April 7, 1961. However, it was easily repelled as the Cuban population rallied to support Castro and the revolution.

Castro then proclaimed his intention to make Cuba a communist society and entered an alliance with the Soviet Union, even placing Soviet nuclear missiles in Cuba. This very nearly led to nuclear war between the United States and the Soviets, but after a tense standoff and naval blockade by the United States, the missiles were withdrawn. Nonetheless, the United States maintained a strict trade embargo on Cuba and restrictions on travel, which still remain in place.

Although Castro remained a national hero for standing up to the United States, the economy did poorly under communism and survived only with support from the Soviet Union, and later from allies such as Venezuela. Castro encouraged thousands of his opponents to flee to the United States, where most settled in Florida. Those who remained in Cuba and dared to be critical of Castro's regime, even once-fellow revolutionaries, ended up in prison or executed. When Fidel grew too ill to rule in 2008, his brother Raul continued as new leader of the Communist regime.

Castro's victory, and his defiance of the United States., inspired other would-be revolutionaries. In the years that followed, his old compatriot Che Guevara developed a new theory of revolutions in which he argued that a small band of guerrillas, a *foco* (focus) of opposition, could overthrow any unjust regime. But this was not true. Castro's band had benefitted from amazing good luck, from the brutality and corruption of Batista's personalist regime, from the Cuban peoples' deep resentment of foreign business and political interference, and the U.S. decision to stop arms shipments. Elsewhere, when aspiring revolutionaries tried to organize *foco* movements against more efficient military regimes, or against regimes that retained U.S. support, they were cut down. Che himself was captured and executed while working with a *foco* group in Bolivia in 1967.

Meanwhile, the Castro regime survived decade after decade, weathering the collapse of the Soviet Union and continuing to draw on Cuban nationalism and resentment of the U.S. embargo to shore up its support. But as in China, Cuba's communist leaders have discovered that it is impossible to grow an economy without some free-market activity. The regime has recently encouraged international tourism and reformed the rules regarding small businesses, banking, real estate, and the markets for cars, computers, and consumer goods. It remains to be seen, however, how fast changes will occur under the conservative guidance of Raul, and what a new generation of leaders might bring.

Chapter 8

Revolutions against dictators: Mexico, Nicaragua, and Iran

The revolutions in Mexico, Nicaragua, and Iran have provided us with some of the most striking characters in the history of revolutions—the bandit leader Pancho Villa; the wily guerrilla leader-turned-president Daniel Ortega; and the forbidding Ayatollah Khomeini. Each led a revolution against modernizing dictatorships, which had become corrupt, personalist regimes.

Personalist rulers tend to alienate elites by using patronage and corruption to grab economic gains for their family members and cronies, while burdening the broader business elite. They also often weaken the military, either distancing it from power or replacing professionals with loyalists, in order to reduce the risk of a military coup. Because their economic policies favor the ruler and his cronies, such regimes often produce uneven growth, inflation, or other economic problems, producing widespread anger against the regime.

Though similar in their origins, revolutions against personalist regimes are quite varied. In Mexico, despite a murderous civil war, it was moderate leaders who triumphed and consolidated the revolution. It was only a decade later that a more radical program of land reforms and nationalization of major industries was carried out. In Nicaragua, the revolutionary regime was unique in giving up power after losing a fair election, barely a decade after

the revolution. Yet in subsequent elections the revolutionary leader
was peacefully returned to power. In Iran, the new revolutionary
regime was an Islamic republic—a novelty in world history and
proof that revolutions can always produce something new.

The Mexican Revolution

After winning its independence from Spain in 1821, Mexico
experienced half a century of political tumult. Military leaders
fought for power, with foreign powers often intervening, until
in 1876 Gen. Porfirio Díaz took control of the country. Díaz
led Mexico for thirty-four years, and although he tolerated no
opposition, he brought a period of stability and economic growth.
As president of Mexico, Díaz promoted foreign investments in
mining, railroads, and export agriculture, all of which led to an
expansion of the middle classes and huge gains in wealth for his
supporters. At the same time, though, foreign interests increased
their control of Mexican land and capital, while the incomes of
peasants, workers, and ranch hands lagged far behind. Peasants
saw their lands being swallowed by expanding commercial estates
(*haciendas*). Many among the middle classes chafed at being
politically excluded by the Díaz dictatorship.

In 1907–9 a sharp downturn in commodity prices afflicted the
mining boomtowns and farms, and spread economic misery
across the country. Francisco Madero, the son of a wealthy landed,
mining, and banking family, started campaigning across Mexico
for democratic elections to unseat Díaz. Madero said that under
Díaz, Mexicans lacked freedom and control of their own fate. As
the 1910 presidential election approached, Madero established
a party and declared his candidacy. But shortly afterwards, Díaz
arrested him and five thousand of his supporters; Díaz then was
reelected president.

Madero escaped across the border to Texas, where he declared
the 1910 election invalid and called on Mexicans to rise up in

revolution. A number of leaders followed his call. These included Emiliano Zapata, a charismatic village leader from Morelos, south of Mexico City, who had been fighting to preserve peasant lands against the encroachments of haciendas. Seeing Madero's campaign as a chance for land reform, Zapata raised a peasant army to fight against Díaz's forces in southern Mexico. Another who followed was Francisco (Pancho) Villa, a former bandit who joined the pro-Madero forces, and later raised his own army from ranch hands and peasants in the north. Yet another was an ambitious senator from northern Mexico, Venustiano Carranza. Unable to defeat the fast-growing revolutionary forces, Díaz resigned, and in 1911 Madero entered Mexico City as a hero.

Madero was elected president with 90 percent of the vote later that year. But his triumph was short lived. In 1912 local rebellions against his regime broke out, financed by former Díaz supporters. Madero also faced opposition from disgruntled popular rebels like Zapata who demanded more radical reforms. Then, in early 1913 Victoriano Huerta, one of Díaz's former generals who had helped to defend Madero against the rebellions and become commander of the Mexican Army, used his soldiers to seize power and had Madero killed. Huerta's actions triggered a new round of civil war. Carranza gathered military forces loyal to Madero to fight against Huerta and restore a constitutional democracy. He appointed Álvaro Obregón, a talented officer who had fought in the defense of Madero in 1912, as General for the northwest. Meanwhile, Zapata and Villa raised their popular armies to fight for land reform and worker's rights.

Following major victories by Villa and Obregón in 1914, Huerta fled Mexico. Carranza now entered Mexico City and took power. Yet the civil wars were far from over. Zapata did not trust Carranza; he seized control of Morelos and carried out land reforms to benefit the peasants. Zapata then forged an agreement with Villa to fight against Carranza and Obregón. Over the next two years, ferocious battles raged across Mexico, with Obregón losing an arm and Villa's forces being pursued by an American force under General Pershing. By 1917, Zapata's and Villa's main forces had been defeated, although skirmishes continued. Zapata was finally trapped and assassinated in 1919. Villa agreed to retire peacefully in 1920 but was assassinated in 1923.

Carranza had gained political support by calling a convention in 1916 to draft a new, democratic constitution. Passed the following year, it permitted workers to form labor unions, prohibited child labor, required equal pay for men and women, and gave the government the right to redistribute land to the poor. Yet Carranza declined to enforce many of these provisions, moving cautiously on economic reforms and resisting radical change. Just before the 1920 elections, Carranza turned on Obregón, who had planned to run for president. This was a fatal mistake; Obregón was popular and turned his forces against Carranza. Now it was time for Carranza to flee. Filling a train with gold from the national treasury, materials from the archives, and thousands of supporters, he headed to Veracruz. But his train was intercepted by Obregón's forces and Carranza was killed. Obregón was then elected president in 1920.

In 1924 Obregón's interior minister Plutarco Elías Calles was elected president, running on a platform promising more land reform and workers' rights. But once in office, he instead focused on increasing restrictions on the Catholic Church, whose central role in Mexico had already been attacked in the Constitution of 1917. Calles saw the Church as an overly wealthy and conservative bastion of superstition and an obstacle to progress; but he underestimated Mexicans' attachment to their clergy and their Catholic faith. From 1926 to 1929, Mexico was rent by the "Cristero" war, with Catholic groups fighting government forces. In 1928 Obregón was again elected president, but before he could take office he was assassinated by a Catholic partisan. In 1929 Calles—then the minister of war but still dominating the government—made peace with the Church. Calles institutionalized his power by founding the National Revolutionary Party. This party—later renamed the Institutional Revolutionary Party, better known by its Spanish initials as the PRI—would go on to dominate Mexican politics for the next seventy-one years.

Carranza, Obregón, and Calles had all been moderate constitutionalists, less interested in land reform and workers' rights than in restoring economic growth. They had taken only limited action to satisfy peasants' and workers' demands, and had continued to allow foreign companies to exploit Mexican resources. In the late 1930s, after the global depression set back Mexico's economy, the revolution entered a second radical phase. Lázaro Cárdenas, elected president in 1934, had Calles and many of Calles's supporters arrested and exiled. Cárdenas believed the revolution had not gone far enough in helping ordinary Mexicans. During his presidency, Cárdenas undertook extensive land reforms, promoted new national labor unions and higher wages for workers, and nationalized the foreign-owned railways and oil industry. Cárdenas took control of Calles's party and solidified its hold on government by developing corporatist alliances with organizations representing peasants, workers, and professionals.

After Cárdenas's presidency, successive leaders ran Mexico as an authoritarian state, with politics dominated by the PRI, and each president handpicking his successor. Only in 2000, after decades of economic growth had expanded the middle class and a series of economic crises in the 1980s and 1990s had undermined support for the PRI, did the party lose a presidential election and Mexico become a true constitutional democracy.

The Nicaraguan Revolution

In 1972 a massive earthquake struck the Nicaraguan capital of Managua. Although no one realized it at the time, the quake not only destroyed much of the city but also marked the beginning of the end for the Somoza dynasty, which had ruled Nicaragua since 1936.

Nicaraguan politics up to the 1920s had been a history of feuding families with private militias and repeated U.S. intervention. In 1926 a civil war erupted between leading families contending for the presidency, and the United States sent the Marines to help keep order. The United States trained and equipped a new Nicaraguan National Guard, which they hoped would defend the constitution after U.S. forces left. But the guard turned out to be loyal mainly to its commander, Gen. Anastasío Somoza García, the American-educated son of a coffee plantation owner.

Augusto César Sandino, who led a guerrilla army in the war, stated that the United States would choose a puppet president to back foreign interests, and vowed not to lay down his arms until all U.S. troops left Nicaragua. Sandino fought the Marines and the National Guard until 1932. Then, under pressure from the Great Depression, the United States agreed to remove its forces after holding new elections, and Sandino agreed to disarm.

But General Somoza did not accept the deal. In 1934 he assassinated Sandino, and two years later he deposed the elected president and seized power. Somoza ruled for twenty years, until he himself was assassinated. He was succeeded by his son Luis Somoza Debayle, who ruled from 1956 until he died in 1967. The presidency then passed to Luis's younger brother, Anastasio Somoza Debayle.

The elder Somoza and his son Luis were clever politicians. They relied on control of the National Guard, of course, but they also courted favor with other prominent families and politicians, encouraging them with judgeships and posts in the legislature and favored treatment for their businesses. The Somozas allied themselves with America against Germany in World War II and then joined America's anticommunist crusade during the Cold War. The Somozas also supported U.S. business interests in Nicaraguan mining, cattle, coffee, and timber.

From 1960 to 1975 Nicaragua's economy grew strongly as the United States sent aid to cement Nicaragua's support in the wake of Cuba's communist revolution, and exports of coffee, cattle, timber, and rubber expanded. But due to rapid population growth (Nicaragua's population doubled from 1950 to 1970), restrictions on union organizing, and increasingly concentrated land-ownership, the benefits of Nicaragua's economic growth went overwhelmingly to the upper-class elites, and inequality thus increased.

In 1961 a small group of Marxists—mostly educated middle-class youth inspired by the revolution in Cuba—formed a movement they named for the Nicaraguan national hero Augusto César Sandino, calling themselves the Sandinista Front for National Liberation (FSLN). Yet they drew little popular support and were hunted down by the National Guard. Many were jailed and tortured by Somoza's troops.

The tide started to turn in the late 1960s. The Catholic Church in Latin America began to follow the tenets of Liberation Theology, which argued that the Church should help improve the lives of the poor and support struggles for human rights. In response several FSLN leaders, including the Ortega brothers, Daniel and Humberto, set aside Marxism and started to build a more diverse anti-Somoza movement that welcomed workers, peasants, businessmen, and clergy.

After the Managua earthquake in 1972, international aid poured in to rebuild the shattered city. Yet the populace and even business elites were shocked to see Somoza and several of his business associates treat this as an opportunity to grow rich. Somoza pocketed most of the reconstruction aid, investing it in his own land-development projects and leaving a third of the city in ruins. National Guard units seized and sold off reconstruction equipment and supplies. In the years following the earthquake, the economy slowed sharply, causing widespread distress to workers and peasants while Somoza and his cronies increased their wealth.

In the mid-1970s, the Ortega brothers masterminded several daring strikes, kidnapping prominent Nicaraguans and ransoming them for funds, prisoner releases, and opportunities to spread their message via the media. Somoza responded by declaring martial law in 1975, sending the National Guard to spread terror in the countryside, and arresting and torturing hundreds of FSLN supporters. Pedro Joaquín Chamorro, editor of the newspaper *La Prensa*, began a campaign to expose the brutality and corruption of the Somoza regime, fanning middle- and upper-class opposition.

In 1977 the new U.S. president Jimmy Carter, who had promised to make defense of human rights a priority, threatened to stop military aid to Nicaragua unless Somoza dropped martial law. Somoza complied and released many of his political prisoners. This gave the FSLN a fresh chance to organize workers in the cities and build up its guerrilla forces in the countryside. Then in January 1978, Chamorro was assassinated, leading to an outpouring of strikes and demonstrations. Aid from other countries in Latin America started to flow to the FSLN.

In the autumn of 1978 Somoza reinstated martial law, and ordered the National Guard to attack urban neighborhoods dominated by FSLN supporters with planes, tanks, and artillery, killing thousands. Business and religious leaders pleaded with President Carter to negotiate a peaceful departure for Somoza and broker a deal with the FSLN, but the talks went nowhere. Even when the United States stopped all military assistance to his government, Somoza refused to leave.

In early 1979, crowds in many cities, including the capital, built barricades and took control of neighborhoods. Somoza ordered the guard to fight back, bombing Managua and shooting thousands, including an American television journalist. In May 1979 the FSLN launched a final offensive with coordinated urban uprisings and guerrilla advances into major cities. The United States and the Organization of American States asked Somoza to resign. The

National Guard, now deprived of ammunition by the United States and demoralized by international support for the FSLN, started to disintegrate. Somoza left the country, and in July 1979 Sandinista fighters took control of Managua as the remnants of the National Guard fled to Honduras.

Even though the FSLN controlled the country, they first sought to rule with a broad coalition, setting up a provisional junta with business leaders and priests, including Chamorro's widow, Violeta, who had taken over *La Prensa*. In the first national elections in 1984, Daniel Ortega was chosen president, and the FSLN won a majority in the legislature. The FSLN immediately nationalized all of the Somoza family's assets.

But the alliance between the Marxist-leaning FSLN and the business and religious communities did not last. The FSLN threatened to nationalize more private lands and businesses. In addition, when Ronald Reagan was elected president of the United States in 1980, he saw the Sandinistas as no different from Cuba. He imposed an economic embargo and gave aid and military support to the former guard members in Honduras to form a "Contra" army to harass the Sandinistas. As the costs of the Contra war rose, people began to look for an alternative. In the 1990 elections, Violeta Chamorro ran against Ortega and was elected president. The FSLN also lost their majority in the legislature, although they retained nearly half the seats.

In the presidential elections of 1996 and 2001, Ortega ran again but lost to moderate candidates backed by the business community. The business leaders soon proved corrupt and did little to improve the lot of the average Nicaraguan. In 2006 Ortega ran again and won this time, and he was reelected with an even larger majority in 2011. Although the FSLN did not accomplish all they sought, as poverty and corruption continued under the various elected regimes, their struggle ended the Somoza dictatorship. And unlike most socialist revolutions, they left Nicaragua with a far more democratic and vigorous civil society.

The Iranian Islamic Revolution

Although Mohammad Reza Shah Pahlavi of Iran claimed to follow in the line of ancient Persian kings, his family had come to power, like the Somozas, in a military coup. The shah's father, Reza Khan, was a general in the Iranian army. In 1921 Reza Khan deposed the shah, and in 1925 took the title of shah (king) for himself.

Although Iran had a Parliament (the *Majles*), Reza gave it little independence and ruled with near absolute power, enriching his family through exploitation of Iran's oil and acquiring extensive landholdings. Reza Shah also began a program of modernization, building railways, promoting education and public health, and banning the veil while promoting Western dress.

When World War II broke out, Reza Shah sought to remain neutral and bar the Allies from using Iran as a supply corridor to Russia. But in 1941 Britain and Russia invaded, deposed the "old" shah, and in exchange for compliance with their demands, allowed his son, Mohammed Reza Pahlevi, to take the throne as the new shah.

In 1951 Mohammad Mossadegh, a popular nationalist, became prime minister. Under his leadership the *Majles* passed a bill to take control of Britain's Anglo-Iranian Oil Company, which produced most of Iran's oil. Mossadegh also demanded that more power be given to the *Majles*. The shah refused, and Mossadegh resigned, calling on the public to support him. Huge protests and strikes arose across the country, and Mossadegh was returned to office with expanded powers. However, Britain responded with an embargo on Iran's oil, hurting the economy and costing Mossadegh public support. In 1953 Britain and the United States had the CIA arrange a coup against Mossadegh that restored the shah to absolute power.

Had the shah then sought to broaden his base of support, he might have ruled in peace. But he became a personalist ruler, following his own vision and tolerating no dissent or restrictions on his power. He sought to limit the power and wealth of the clergy by breaking up their estates, but peasants who were intended to benefit from the land reforms often received too little land to support a family. Millions of peasants moved to the cities, where they were drawn into the mosque networks run by the now resentful clergy, and supported by the traditional merchants of the bazaars (*bazaaris*). Supporting OPEC in driving up the world price of oil, the shah spent and borrowed wildly to acquire the latest weapons (supplied by the United States) and to force a modern reconstruction of his country. Yet his spending unleashed rampant inflation that undermined the welfare of even the middle class and industrial workers. The shah chose to blame the *bazaaris* for raising prices, imprisoning many and thus earning their fierce enmity. By the 1970s the shah had managed to turn virtually every sector of Iranian society—the clergy, the peasantry, the urban poor, the working classes, the *bazaaris*, and the professional middle class—against him.

The shah retained power by use of his secret service, harsh repression, and support from the United States. But in 1977 President Jimmy Carter warned the shah to loosen his grip and respect human rights. This allowed strikes and public demonstrations to challenge the shah.

Many groups were involved in the opposition—communists who had influence with oil and industrial workers, liberal intellectuals and students who wanted to replace the shah's dictatorship with democracy, traditional merchants and peasants who hated the shah's aggressive support for western dress and culture, nationalists who wanted to end U.S. influence, and various groups of clergy. The most influential critic, however, was the Ayatollah Ruhollah Khomeini. Khomeini had been exiled for his criticism of the shah since 1964, spending most of his time in the Shi'a holy city of Najaf in Iraq. While in exile, Khomeini relentlessly criticized

8. Ayatollah Ruhollah Khomeini, Supreme Leader of the Islamic Republic of Iran.

the shah for betraying Iran and Islam; he developed a plan for an Islamic Republic, which would embrace Islamic virtue, democracy, and Iranian nationalism. Khomeini's sermons and plans were spread throughout Iran on smuggled cassette tapes.

Khomeini encouraged massive peaceful protests. He believed the shah's soldiers would not sustain attacks on ordinary Iranians conducting peaceful protests. At first, this proved wrong. When protests spread throughout the country in 1978, the shah responded with force, killing hundreds. But Khomeini exploited the situation by proclaiming them martyrs and calling for new protests to mourn for them. This created a cycle of ever larger protests, leading to "Black Friday" on September 8, 1978, when the shah declared martial law and his forces killed thousands of unarmed demonstrators. Workers responded with massive strikes that shut down the oil industry, devastating the economy. President Carter then told the shah he would not support the use of force. In January 1979, after weeks of massive street demonstrations, the shah departed for Egypt; in February, Khomeini returned to Iran.

In October, the shah traveled to New York for cancer treatment, causing outrage in Iran. With Khomeini denouncing the United States as the "Great Satan" and "enemy of Islam," and fearing that the United States might act to restore the shah as it had in 1953, on November 4 thousands of Iranians stormed the U.S. Embassy. Sixty-six Americans were taken hostage and held until President Carter left office in January 1981.

In September 1980, fearing the spread of Iran's radical Shi'a republican ideology and thinking Iran had been weakened by the revolution, Iraq invaded. The crisis allowed Khomeini and the clergy to tighten their grip on power. In 1981 the liberal Irani president Abolhassan Bani Sadr was removed from power and fled to France; by then, many of the leftist supporters of the revolution had been outlawed, with many killed while in prison. The presidency eventually went to another cleric, Seyed Ali Khamenei. Iran relied on human waves of attacks by teenage soldiers, stiffened by the newly formed Revolutionary Guard, to repel the invasion. But hundreds of thousands became martyrs in a war that lasted until 1988.

In 1989 Ayatollah Khomeini died and was succeeded as supreme leader by Seyed Ali Khamenei. Since 1989 Iran's leadership has been divided between relative pragmatists and more conservative Islamists. Under the reformist president Mohammad Khatami from 1997 to 2005, the revolution pursued a more moderate path, with students and several prominent ayatollahs supporting the pragmatists. However, the election of Mahmoud Ahmadinejad as president in 2005 marked a turn back toward a more confrontational Islamist regime.

In 2009 a coalition of pragmatists supported a reform candidate to run against Ahmadinejad, and elections seemed poised to swing the country back toward moderation. Yet in what appeared to be a blatant rigging of the results, Ahmadinejad was declared the winner. Millions participated in peaceful protests in Tehran (the so-called Green Revolution), challenging the outcome. However, Khamenei, the Revolutionary Guards, and the conservative clergy were resolute, and the guards and militia put down the protests. Iran continued its pursuit of nuclear technology, defying economic sanctions that were imposed and tightened by Europe and the United States.

The tide seemed to swing back toward reform in 2013, when an ayatollah from the pragmatist camp, Hassan Rouhani, was elected President with an overwhelming majority of the popular vote. The Iranian people thus had voted for change. But as Rouhani took his oath of office, Iran remained in a hostile relationship with the United States, and was continuing its support of Islamist groups throughout the Middle East and expanding its capacities to produce nuclear materials. Iran's regime maintains that all of its actions, including pursuit of nuclear power, are solely for peaceful purposes; yet its involvement in revolutionary conflicts in Syria and Bahrain, and its support of Lebanese Hezbollah, Iraqi, Afghan and other Shi'a groups, all suggest a strategic struggle in which Shi'a Iran sees itself competing with Sunni countries for leadership of the greater Middle East. Iran's zeal as the home of a visionary Islamic revolution may thus not be entirely played out.

Chapter 9

Color revolutions: The Philippines, Eastern Europe and the USSR, and Ukraine

Victims hanging from lamp posts, guerrilla warfare, terror, civil wars, international conflicts: these hallmarks of revolution lead us to view them as violent events. Yet violence is not the only way to overthrow a government. Disruptive nonviolent actions have also toppled regimes. These include marches and general strikes, occupation of public spaces, and refusals to obey government orders. Also vital are efforts to win over soldiers and actions to expose corruption and malfeasance. Such efforts can succeed if they deprive the government of resources, lead the military to defect, build a broad coalition of opponents, and cause foreign powers to abandon or pressure the government.

Nonviolent resistance works best where rulers depend on support from a democratic foreign power that will neither tolerate ruthless actions against a peaceful opposition nor pay a high price to back the existing regime. Gandhi's success in leading the Indian Independence movement against Britain relied on both the British public's repugnance at peaceful protestors being brutally treated and the high costs to Britain of Gandhi's followers boycotting British goods. The shah of Iran was similarly vulnerable when President Jimmy Carter of the United States (upon whom the shah depended for weapons and credit), insisted that the shah call off his dreaded secret service (SAVAK) and permit the opposition to conduct peaceful demonstrations against his rule.

Where a loyal and determined military supports a financially strong and independent government, nonviolent resistance will usually fail, succumbing to harsh repression. Such was the fate of the attempted Green Revolution against clerical rule in Iran in 2009, the pro-democracy revolt in Burma in 1988, and the Tiananmen Square revolt in China in 1989.

Yet since the mid-1980s, several factors have improved the prospects for nonviolent resistance to overturn regimes. First, global norms have moved strongly in the direction of requiring elections for regimes to claim legitimacy. Even dictatorships have felt the need to hold elections, though they often will manipulate the results to produce victories. From the Philippines to Ukraine, protests over flawed elections have become powerful movements that forced regime change. Second, new mass media—including cell phones, YouTube, Facebook, Twitter, other social media, and international cable television—have made it easier for the opposition to acquire and disseminate evidence of regime abuses. Third, the rise of an international network of activists to provide training in nonviolent resistance methods has empowered opposition movements. Finally, the end of the Cold War has reduced the willingness of the United States and other powers to intervene militarily to keep rulers in power against the wishes of their own people.

As a result, nonviolent revolutions have predominated in recent years. Sometimes called "democratic" or "electoral" revolutions (when the mass protests stemmed from election campaigns), they are more commonly called "color revolutions" after the symbols adopted by the opposition in these events, such as the yellow ribbons worn in the Philippines and the orange ones in Ukraine. Other recent nonviolent revolutions include the anticommunist revolutions in the USSR and Eastern Europe, such as the "Velvet Revolution" in Czechoslovakia (1989); the "Bulldozer Revolution" in Serbia (2000); the "Rose Revolution" in Georgia (2003); the "Tulip Revolution" in Kyrgyzstan (2005); and the "Jasmine Revolution" in Tunisia (2011).

The Philippines' "People Power" Revolution

In 1965 Ferdinand Marcos, a brilliant lawyer with a beauty queen wife and the credentials of a war hero (which later turned out to be fabricated), won the Philippine presidency. Once in power, he made his wife, Imelda, the governor of Manila, gave high posts to his brother and sister, appointed his cousin head of National Intelligence, and handed out lucrative rights to timber, precious metals, and coconut plantations to his friends. The Marcos family grew immensely rich; Imelda was infamous for her collection of more than three thousand pairs of designer shoes.

Yet Marcos was also a shrewd ruler, bribing Congress to support him, controlling the media, and spending lavishly on roads, bridges, and stadiums to gain popular appeal. In a campaign marked by vote-buying, violence, and suspected fraud, he was reelected president in 1969. In September 1972 Marcos declared martial law, justifying his actions by pointing to student riots and a growing communist insurgency in the countryside, including violence staged by his own intelligence officers. He announced that elections would be suspended indefinitely, then ordered the arrest of his political opponents, including the popular senator Benigno "Ninoy" Aquino. Aquino was sentenced to death for rebellion and spent eight years in prison before being granted medical leave to have surgery in the United States.

Marcos remained popular for the first few years of martial law, as he redistributed land from wealthy landowners to poor peasants and disarmed private armies (although mainly those of his opponents). But in the late 1970s, as the economy began to stagnate and poverty and unemployment increased, the Marcoses' lavish lifestyle became more repugnant and their popularity faded.

From 1975 on, Marcos relied more on the army, where politically loyal officers were given large raises and promotions ahead of more professional soldiers. Marcos's opponents were increasingly subject to arrest and torture. Marcos also benefited from divisions among the elites, as the wealthy businessmen and landowners who resented Marcos's takeover of the economy and longed for a return to a democracy could never agree on a leader or common strategy to oppose him.

Then in 1983, Marcos took the lethal step that was his undoing. In August Ninoy Aquino returned to the Philippines. He was shot and killed the moment he stepped off the plane onto Philippine soil. Aquino's martyrdom produced two trends fatal to Marcos—the unification of his opponents and rifts within the military.

Manila's Cardinal Jaime Sin encouraged the opposition to rally around Ninoy's widow, Corazon "Cory" Aquino. Cardinal Sin and several religious orders invited a pacifist organization, the International Fellowship of Reconciliation, to train union leaders, professionals, students, and clergy in the techniques of civil resistance. At the same time, the defense minister Juan Ponce Enrile and junior officers formed the Reform the Armed Forces Movement (RAM), which began meeting with the opposition. Corruption in the military also repelled Gen. Fidel Ramos, a West Point graduate who was passed over for promotion in favor of Fabian Ver, a favorite of Marcos who had masterminded Ninoy's killing.

After Ninoy's death, anxious businessmen began to move their money out of the country. Ninoy's funeral procession drew hundreds of thousands of mourners, and anti-Marcos protests and strikes went on for months. By late 1983, economic growth had fallen to just 1.1 percent, as against an average of 6.4 percent per year in the early 1970s. In October Marcos announced that the Philippines could not pay its debts and needed to reschedule them. The debt crisis triggered shortages of imported oil and food, and inflation leaped to 50 percent. Even Marcos's friends in the United States—whose largest air and naval bases in the Pacific were located just fifty miles from Manila—urged him to shore up his legitimacy.

Marcos called National Assembly elections in 1984. Printing millions of fresh pesos to use as bribes, dominating the national media, and ordering security forces to intimidate voters, Marcos again led his party to victory. Flush with success, Marcos scheduled a new presidential election for February 1986, certain that he could control the outcome.

But this time the opposition was better prepared. With support from Cardinal Sin, who encouraged priests and nuns to lead local chapters, the National Citizens Movement for Free Elections (NAMFREL) organized half a million volunteers to monitor polling places and guard ballot boxes throughout the country. Their polling made it clear that Corazon Aquino had won a resounding victory. Nonetheless, when the official vote count was released on February 15, Marcos was declared the winner. The final tally was condemned as false by the Bishops Conference of the Philippines, American election observers, and even several dozen Election Commission tabulators who had walked out after seeing their vote counts being drastically altered.

The next day, Cory Aquino addressed a rally of two million people in Manila and called for a civil disobedience campaign to oust Marcos. Meanwhile, Enrile and Ramos were planning a military coup. They set up their base in Camp Aguinaldo on February 22 with several hundred RAM soldiers. That night, Cardinal Sin broadcast an appeal on Catholic Radio asking Philippine citizens to aid the rebel soldiers. By the next morning, hundreds of thousands of Filipinos had surrounded the camp to offer their support.

Marcos sent a tank battalion to crush the revolt. But the soldiers found a well-organized, cheerful crowd, trained and disciplined to remain nonviolent. In the front line, nuns kneeled with rosaries in front of the tanks, while pregnant women, grandmothers, and children offered food and water to the soldiers. Despite orders to move forward and use their weapons, the soldiers refused to kill unarmed, peaceful civilians. Instead they began to join the crowd. Over the next few days, nearly 80 percent of the army defected. Television workers refused to broadcast statements from Marcos. On February 25, realizing that his power was gone, Marcos took the advice of the U.S. administration to leave, and he boarded a plane for Hawaii. People power had won.

Anticommunist revolutions in Eastern Europe and the Soviet Union

In 1944, after pushing the German forces back to Berlin, the Soviet Army occupied all of Eastern Europe. The Soviet Union then supported local communist parties in taking over the governments of Czechoslovakia, Bulgaria, Romania, Poland, and Hungary. They also turned their occupied portion of Germany into the new communist-ruled state of East Germany, excepting only the western portion of Berlin, still occupied by the Allies. The changes were not always accepted; the Soviets had to send tanks to crush peaceful attempts to overturn communist regimes in Hungary in 1956 and Czechoslovakia in 1968. They also had to build walls across Berlin and around East Germany to keep East Germans from fleeing west. Nonetheless, backed by their secret police and the Soviet Army and controlling the economy, the media, travel, and employment, the communist regimes kept their iron grip, tolerating no dissent.

At first, these regimes enjoyed some economic success, rebuilding from the devastation of World War II. Their centralized, party-run economies aimed for greater production of steel, tractors, cement, oil, and weapons. Copying and adapting designs from the West, they built powerful heavy industrial economies. But the lack of any market incentives or individual freedoms eventually undermined their production. Ever-larger investments simply produced ever-larger piles of substandard steel, tractors that broke down and lay idle for want of spare parts, and stockpiles of oil, cement, and other goods produced to meet a plan rather than market demand. Innovative high-quality consumer goods remained scarce and had to be imported. Agriculture was a major failure, never achieving the productivity reached in Europe, the United States, or Japan, and keeping pace with America's military spending and technological progress was more and more costly and difficult.

With Stalin's death in 1956, communist leaders saw the need for some reforms. For three decades, they sought to maintain tight political control while meeting consumer demand by increasingly importing items from the West. Yet by the late 1970s, this strategy produced enormous corruption, as party leaders controlled access to desired imported goods. Spending on imports also led to spiraling state debts. When Mikhail Gorbachev was elected the youngest ever general secretary of the Communist Party of the Soviet Union (CPSU) in 1985, he already had a plan for major changes.

Gorbachev aimed to root out corruption and advance a new generation of communist leaders. His chosen tools were twofold: *glasnost*—opening up information flows to expose the wrongs of corrupt CPSU leaders, and *perestroika*—restructuring government to introduce more democracy. Gorbachev believed that given a choice, people would choose leaders bent on efficiency, reform, and economic improvement.

Unfortunately for Gorbachev, by the late 1980s all of the communist economies were in serious decline. Discontent among workers over stagnant pay, elite corruption, and living conditions that lagged far behind the West was rampant. Intellectuals and workers throughout Eastern Europe's communist bloc demanded their own versions of *glasnost* and *perestroika*, and Gorbachev made it clear that the Soviet military was not available to intervene.

In Poland, the Solidarity movement of workers, intellectuals, and clergy, led by the skilled shipyard workers of Gdansk, was driven underground by martial law in 1981 but revived in the mid-1980s. After major strikes in 1988, the Polish government agreed to hold new elections, believing it could still win the majority of seats. In fact, Solidarity won every seat it contested, while Communist Party candidates could not even obtain the 50 percent of votes needed to win uncontested seats. In 1989 the new Solidarity-led parliament took control of the government. Lech Wałęsa, leader of the shipyard workers and co-founder of Solidarity, was elected president in 1990.

Throughout 1989, in Hungary and Czechoslovakia marches and demonstrations filled the streets and squares with hundreds of thousands of people calling for change. Deprived of Soviet support, deserted by intellectuals, and reluctant to use their military against peaceful protestors, the leaders of these countries agreed to hold elections that would turn the communist parties out of office. In Bulgaria, a reform faction in the Communist Party itself took control of part of the army and the Politburo, and led a transition to democracy. And in Romania, ruled by the megalomaniac Nicolae Ceauçescu, crowds in the capital and then the army turned on the dictator, who was captured and executed.

In East Germany, by October 1989 hundreds of thousands of the best and brightest had taken advantage of the changes in Eastern Europe to flee to West Germany via Hungary. After weeks of massive public demonstrations in Leipzig, East Berlin, and other cities, during which many units in the armed forces defected or told their superiors they would not fire on German citizens, the government gave in and allowed free movement to the West. On November 9, thousands of citizens swarmed the checkpoints and joyously tore down the Berlin Wall. In the following weeks Communist control disintegrated, and by 1990 East Germany itself had ceased to exist, having reunited with West Germany.

Yet the most dramatic changes occurred in the Soviet Union. In 1986 an explosion at the Chernobyl nuclear plant sprayed large

9. Crowds in Wenceslas Square, Prague, Czechoslovakia, creating the Velvet Revolution, 1989.

parts of the Ukraine with radioactive fallout, gravely discrediting the CPSU. Instead of supporting reform-minded communist leaders, people began to back nationalist anticommunist politicians. From Azerbaijan to Estonia, millions of people took part in demonstrations demanding greater autonomy—and even secession—for the Soviet Union's national republics. In 1987 Boris Yelstin, a popular reform leader in Russia, was removed from the Communist Party's ruling Politburo; in June 1991 he was elected president of the Russian Federation. Gorbachev, who was still general secretary of the CPSU, grew uneasy with what his reforms had unleashed and tried to crack down on these movements. But by spring of 1991, after a wave of strikes throughout the country and demonstrations by hundreds of thousands of pro-democracy protestors in Moscow, he retreated, and proposed a new constitution that would give far-reaching autonomy to the national republics.

This was too much for hardliners in the Communist Party, the military, and the secret police, who plotted a coup to remove

Gorbachev from office and reverse his reforms. In August 1991, the coup plotters held Gorbachev in his summer home in Crimea while they tried to take control of Moscow. They seized the Kremlin and major television stations, and sent tanks into the streets. Yet they failed to arrest Yeltsin, who called for his supporters to gather at the Russian Parliament building, where they began to build barricades and distributed flyers denouncing the coup. On August 20, the coup leaders ordered paratroopers, three tank companies, and a helicopter squadron to attack the Parliament building. But key military officers refused and ordered their troops away from the building. The coup then quickly fell apart as the population and much of the military rallied to Yelstin as president of the Russian Federation. When Gorbachev returned to Moscow, he found he had been effectively replaced by Yeltsin as the national leader. On August 24, he resigned as CPSU general secretary, and over the following months, the Soviet Union dissolved. One after another, from September through December, the former Soviet Socialist Republics voted to become independent states.

The Orange Revolution in Ukraine

The collapse of the Soviet Union did not produce the same outcomes everywhere. In Eastern Europe, where most countries had prior experience with democracy before World War II, the new regimes moved toward becoming liberal constitutional democracies, aided by the promise of future integration into the European Union. By 2013 all of the former communist countries of Eastern Europe (excepting Albania and some former parts of Yugoslavia), along with the former Soviet Republics of Latvia, Lithuania, and Estonia, had met these conditions and been accepted into the EU.

Russia itself, however, fell back into authoritarian ways. The Communist Party was gone, but Yeltsin proved to be an erratic leader. Under his presidency, Russia was rocked by rebellions and economic crises. He was succeeded by a former KGB officer,

Vladimir Putin, who promised to continue modernizing Russia while also strengthening the government. Putin did solidify the government and restore the economy, but he did so by reaching an accommodation with several of the wealthy "oligarchs" who had acquired huge portions of Russia's natural resources and economy under Yeltsin, in return for their political loyalty.

In the other former Soviet Republics in Central Asia and the Caucasus, a similar pattern prevailed, with former communist strong men emerging as presidents, using patronage and corruption to maintain power while investing—with various degrees of success—in economic development.

The people of Ukraine had hoped for a better outcome. In 1994 Leonid Kuchma, an engineer and early critic of the Communist Party, was elected president on a platform of economic reforms. During his second term in office, though, he was implicated in varied crimes and corruption, including the brutal murder of a journalist. Rather than seek a third term he backed his prime minister, Viktor Yanukovich, for president in 2004. His main opponent was Viktor Yushchenko, a former prime minister who led a coalition of reformers including Yulia Tymoshenko.

The election was fiercely contested. Kuchma and Yanukovich used their control of the government and media to intimidate the opposition. Yushchenko was poisoned under mysterious circumstances; although badly disfigured, he survived and returned to the race. The first round of the election produced no clear winner, so a runoff was held on November 21. Exit polls showed a clear win for Yushchenko, but television reports showed Yanukovich with a surprising lead. Additional votes for Yanukovich had suddenly materialized from various regions, pushing turnout to more than 90 percent of the voters in those regions and over 90 percent of those voters apparently opted for the regime's favorite. Allegations of fraud quickly spread, and supporters of Yushchenko began to protest.

On November 22, protestors began to pour into Maidan, the main square in Kiev, Ukraine's capital, wearing orange ribbons for the color of Yuschenko's campaign posters, and calling for a fair count of the vote. Over the next few days, the crowds grew to nearly a million. Yushchenko declared himself the true president of Ukraine and called for a general strike. Local councils voted to refuse to recognize the false election results. The military and security forces started to fragment, many units declaring for Yushchenko; with the security forces so divided, Kuchma did not dare order them to put down the protests. Still, Yanukovich refused to concede. For the next ten days, despite subzero weather, hundreds of thousands of protesters continued to turn out in many of the major cities to protest what they considered a stolen election.

On December 3, the Supreme Court declared the runoff election invalid due to fraud and called for new elections. These were held on December 26 with more than twelve thousand election monitors, many from overseas, observing the polls. Yushchenko won by a clear margin of 52 percent to 44 percent. He was inaugurated as president in January 2005, and appointed Tymoshenko as his prime minister.

Nonviolent revolutions have generally led to more democratic regimes and have avoided the huge economic and human costs of ideologically driven revolutions. Yet color revolutions do not always have happy endings. Especially in countries with little prior history of democracy, developing the trust and institutional frameworks for good governance takes time. New leaders often face a legacy of weak institutions, divided elites, and a restive population.

In the Philippines, Cory Aquino managed to preserve democracy against several attempted military coups. Yet she could not achieve desired land reforms, nor could she curb the influence and corruption of wealthy elites. Aquino was succeeded by Fidel Ramos, whose term started with an economic boom. By its end, however, he was mired in the Asian economic collapse of 1997–98 and accusations of corruption. Ramos was then succeeded by Joseph Estrada, who was impeached for corruption, and followed by Gloria Macapagal-Arroyo, who was arrested for criminal electoral fraud.

In Russia, Vladimir Putin has been in power as president or prime minister continually since 1999 and since his election on March 2012 he is set to continue as president at least until 2018. His most vigorous opponents have been marginalized or imprisoned, while critical journalists have been found murdered. Rampant corruption continues to weaken the economy and undermine the legitimacy of the government.

In Ukraine, Yushchenko spent his presidency in fruitless power struggles with his former ally Yulia Tymoshenko. By 2006 Yanukovich had returned as prime minister, and members of Parliament were shifting their allegiance from Yushchenko to the opposition. In the 2010 presidential election, in which Yanukovich, Yushchenko, and Tymoshenko all ran, Yushchenko received less than 6 percent of the vote, with Yanukovich emerging as the winner. Once in office, Yanukovich restricted press freedoms and put Tymoshenko in jail, prosecuting her for abuse of office and other crimes. It was almost as if the Orange Revolution had not occurred.

As these episodes show, making a revolution is one thing, and one that can occur with surprising speed. Creating a stable democracy is quite another, and may take years or even decades to accomplish. Most of the countries that have had "color' revolutions have not made a swift and certain transition to democracy. Instead, they have had to struggle with corrupt elites who retained their economic power, weak political parties, unreliable judicial systems, and factional struggles. In many of them some backsliding and authoritarian tendencies have emerged. Even color revolutions thus conform to the general pattern of revolutions, in which the fall of the old regime is only the start of a revolutionary process that may take several years or even decades to fully unfold.

Chapter 10
The Arab Revolutions of 2011: Tunisia, Egypt, Libya, and Syria

In February 2013, Zine El Abidine Ben Ali, president of Tunisia for twenty-four years, was in exile in Saudi Arabia, having been tried in absentia and sentenced to life in prison. Hosni Mubarak, president of Egypt for almost thirty years, was under arrest in a military hospital, awaiting retrial for the killing of protestors. Moammar Gaddafi, who ruled Libya for forty-two years, was dead, killed by the rebels who overthrew his regime. Bashar al-Assad, whose family led Syria for forty-three years, was under siege, having lost control of large portions of his country, with the major cities of Aleppo and Damascus under assault.

The sudden collapse of these regimes startled the world. These revolutions have just begun, and it is too soon to say how they will end. But it is not too soon to draw lessons from how they arose.

Tunisia: from immolation to revolution

It is a myth that the Arab revolutions appeared out of nowhere, spontaneously erupting from a peaceful and tightly controlled region. All across the Arab world, similar discontents were building, and strikes and protests had occurred throughout the previous decade.

Arab societies have one of the highest population growth rates of any middle-income region. This produced a huge and ambitious youth bulge, while also reducing the land and water available to farmers. Egypt, Tunisia, Libya, and Syria had all followed the pattern laid down by the Arab socialist leader Gamel Abdel Nasser in the 1950s, aiming to win support by providing generous subsidies for education, food, fuel, and other necessities, and promising government jobs for college graduates. But rapid population growth, combined with the highest dependence on grain imports in the world, rendered these programs increasingly expensive and impractical. By the early 1990s governments started to slash subsidies. In 2008, food riots burst out in Tunisia and Egypt following a spike in food prices; another such spike was underway in 2010. Wages for much of the population lagged behind prices, and while the Arab economies grew by recruiting foreign capital they failed to create sufficient jobs: youth unemployment in the Arab nations was the highest in the world, at around 25 percent. In an exceptional twist, unemployment was highest among the best educated, who expected professional or government jobs but often waited years to find one.

Tunisia had made great strides in educating its youth, but outside of the capital of Tunis, especially in the south, poverty remained widespread and opportunities were few. Resentment increasingly focused on the personalist regime of Ben Ali, whose family was notorious for corruption. Under his rule, the gains from economic growth were channeled to an ever-smaller circle of cronies, while the broader business community bristled at his family's constant demands for payoffs.

As Ben Ali found it harder to rely on broad economic growth or subsidies to retain popular support, his police grew increasingly intrusive and domineering. It was police tormenting a young fruit-seller, Mohammed Bouazizi, in the small southern town of Sidi Bouzid, confiscating his cart and humiliating him, that led to his self-immolation on December 17, 2010 in front of the local police station. Bouazizi's actions resonated among Tunisians who keenly felt the lack of opportunities and constant harassment under Ben Ali's rule.

When a crowd gathered the next day at the police station, the regime responded by firing into the crowd, killing several, and then sought to seal up the protests by blockading roads and censoring the media. But it was no longer simple to keep these events hidden. While the regime exercised strict censorship over national television, radio, newspapers, and most internet sites, it treated Facebook as simply a social outlet and left it alone. Because Tunisia had a relatively large middle class, the percentage of Facebook users among young people was the highest in North Africa. News of the events in Sidi Bouzid and the brutality of the police response spread rapidly online, soon reaching Al-Jazeera, which broadcast it throughout the Arab world.

Riots spread quickly through Tunisia's southern towns. As the regime responded with further acts of repression, which were also broadcast on Facebook and satellite television, anger flamed across the country. A remarkable array of organizations stepped forward to support protests against the regime. The Tunisian General Labor Union, which had been organizing smaller strikes for years among miners, teachers, and other workers, now organized national strikes in major cities. Thousands of internet activists adopted revolutionary personas on Facebook and Twitter; lawyers, journalists, and even rap musicians openly criticized the regime.

The international news media painted the struggle in Tunisia as pitting an internet-savvy but much abused population against a greedy and corrupt ruler. Under these conditions, neither France nor the United States, Ben Ali's traditional allies, would lift a finger to help him. It helped that Islamists were absent from Tunisia's revolts, since Ben Ali had crushed the major Islamist party, Ennahda, and exiled its leaders. With no Islamist threat in sight, the Western world was happy to root for youthful protestors against the aging dictator.

By early January, it was clear that Ben Ali's only hope of survival was to use the army to restore order. However, General Rachid Ammar told Ben Ali that the army was a professional force that would not shoot at Tunisian citizens. On January 14, 2011, less than a month after Bouazizi's desperate act, Ben Ali and his family fled to Saudi Arabia.

Egypt: the pharaoh falls

As satellite networks carried the Tunisian protests across the Arab world, popular despair and resentment against other aging dictators gave way to hope and plans for similar protests. Still, other Arab rulers felt certain that revolution would not spread to their countries. Egypt's foreign minister dismissed the idea as "nonsense." After all, the Mubarak regime had a vast police force and highly professional military. In addition, having been a key bulwark against Islamist movements and maintained peace with Israel, Mubarak had always enjoyed strong American support. Moreover, Egypt's military was deeply invested in the regime. Every president since Nasser had toppled Egypt's monarchy in 1952 had come from the ranks of its officers, and the military had huge investments in tourism, retailing, real estate, and other sectors of the Egyptian economy.

Yet Egypt's regime too proved vulnerable. President Mubarak had been in power so long, and seemed so determined to hand power to his son, Gamal, that people jokingly referred to him as the "last pharaoh." More importantly, Gamal was *not* a member of the military. Rather, he was at the center of a small group of billionaires who had built huge fortunes by exploiting government connections and foreign investment in oil, steel, and banking. Military leaders looked with anxiety on the young civilian heir apparent, wondering if he would respect and maintain their reputation, key national role, and economic empire.

Protest in Egypt was not novel. In 2008, the April 6 youth movement had staged protests that were put down by the regime. The

10. Egypt's President Hosni Mubarak as Pharaoh.

regime reacted harshly to any opposition, and youth activists were frequently jailed. One, Khaled Said, had been beaten to death by police in Alexandria in June 2010. Pictures of his horrifically beaten face circulated on Facebook, creating an online community "We Are All Khaled Said," which built a large network of anti-Mubarak sympathizers. But most Egyptians remained passive.

On January 25, 2011, anti-Mubarak forces organized a protest on the national holiday of "Police Day." The regime was well prepared, with Tahrir Square and other central places tightly patrolled by security forces. What differed in the days following January 25 was not the initial protest but the willingness of vast numbers of ordinary Egyptians to join the vanguard of youth protestors.

Three factors contributed to this change. First, Egypt had held a parliamentary election in December 2010. In 2005, Muslim Brotherhood candidates running as independents (their party was officially banned) had won eighty-eight seats. This time, Mubarak was determined that the Brotherhood candidates would fail miserably, and he exerted every means—arrests, media campaigns, and attacks on their financial resources—to insure that nearly every seat in Parliament was won by his party or his allies. Mubarak extinguished any hope of reform through elections, leaving only protest as a way to achieve change. Second, experts in nonviolent civil resistance from Serbia's Otpor! youth movement, veterans of the nonviolent revolution that drove Slobodan Milošević from power, had trained members of Egypt's April 6 youth movement. They taught the organizers of the January 25 protest the importance of maintaining disciplined nonviolence, and appealing to soldiers and police as friends and countrymen. Third, and by far most important, the example of Tunisia, where street protests had just driven Ben Ali from power, was a beacon to Egyptians. If Tunisians could do this, certainly they could too.

On January 25, people in Cairo began converging on Tahrir Square from all directions, the crowds quickly swelling to tens of thousands. An even larger crowd formed on the Corniche in Alexandria. For the next four days, fierce fighting arose between police and the people for control of public spaces. The revolution did not remain wholly peaceful—police stations and prisons were burned, and protestors attacked police. But by January 28, the police were in retreat; the vast number of people and their determination to hold their ground was simply too great for the police to overcome. It would require the army's tanks and helicopters to clear the squares.

On the evening of January 28, the military was ordered into Tahrir Square. Yet they refused to fire on fellow Egyptians. Soldiers took up positions around the square but took no action against the protestors camped there. As the streets rang with cries that "The

Army and the People are one hand," the Muslim Brotherhood now joined the opposition, committing its organization and manpower to the cause.

The refusal of the army to disperse the crowds created an open-ended crisis. Both the United States and the Egyptian military, who had been in constant talks, were seeking a peaceful transition. But President Mubarak refused to step down. The protestors set up tents and barricades, determined to occupy Tahrir until Mubarak was gone.

On February 10, amid expectations that he would resign, President Mubarak gave a long, rambling speech in which he again insisted he would stay in power until his term ended in September. The next day, massive strikes paralyzed the country from Alexandria to upper Egypt and from Cairo to Suez. Seeing order dissolving, the military removed Mubarak from office. The Supreme Council of the Armed Forces took over the government, promising to return power to a civilian regime once new elections for Parliament and president were held.

Libya: the death of a tyrant

Muammar Gaddafi, who had come to power in a military coup in 1969, was the ultimate personalist ruler. Having nationalized the oil industry, he had little use for formal government. Instead, he used his vast petro-fortune to create a family-led, patronage-run state according to his own bizarre philosophy of *Jamahiriyah*, in which Libya was to be a revolutionary state run by General People's Committees. In practice, Gaddafi made all state decisions and ruled by decree.

Gaddafi fancied himself an Arab socialist and nationalist; he provided subsidies for the poor and expanded secondary and university education. But as in other personalist states, he directed economic benefits mainly to his family and close supporters, leaving the majority of the population with stagnant wages and high unemployment.

In February 2011, Libyan youth called for peaceful pro-democracy protests. The largest took place in the eastern city of Benghazi, whose population historically had often been at odds with the western region and its capital, Tripoli. Gaddafi immediately sought to crush the protests. The army was ordered to shoot protestors on sight, and hundreds were killed in the first week.

Why was the army so much more effective in Libya than in Tunisia or Egypt? In fact, Libya's professional army, just like those of Tunisia and Egypt, chose not to fire on their countrymen. Most defected to the rebels, melted away, or stayed in their barracks. But Libya was unlike Tunisia and Egypt in two respects. First, it was an oil power, giving Gaddafi huge revenues that he directly controlled. He used this wealth to create a private army of mercenaries from sub-Saharan Africa more than twice as large as the official, professional army; these units had no compunction about killing rebel Libyans. Second, Libya remained to a significant extent a tribal society, not a nation. Special "regime protection units" commanded by Gaddafi's sons and recruited mainly from his own tribe were especially loyal, willing to fight to the end against Libyans from other regions.

In Benghazi, the professional military chose to stay in their barracks, and by February 20 the protestors were able to overcome the police and take charge of the city. But elsewhere in Libya, Gaddafi's tanks, artillery, and air power pounded cities into submission, starting in Tripoli and advancing quickly eastward past the oil centers of Ras Lanuf and Brega and toward Benghazi. Gaddafi and his son Saif threatened to kill everyone who had joined the rebellion in Benghazi, saying that "people who don't love me don't deserve to live." By early March, with thousands already dead, Gaddafi's forces were poised to inflict a massacre to recover Benghazi.

Thanks to satellite television and social media, the whole world was watching and sympathizing with the rebels. On March 18 the UN Security Council passed a resolution authorizing the use of force to stop the killing. NATO air strikes immediately began attacking Gaddafi's artillery and tanks on the ground, and sweeping his planes and helicopters from the sky.

Once NATO entered the war against Gaddafi—for it was now a full-blown civil war—the rebels gained legitimacy and began to mobilize more effectively. In late March they began a series of counterattacks under cover of NATO air power. In the next few months, the rebels retook the major oil centers on Libya's central coast, while Gaddafi was weakened by a steady stream of defections. In late July, Berbers in the Western Mountains opened a second front, attacking toward Tripoli from the south while the Benghazi-led rebels attacked from the east. In August, the double-pronged attack produced major advances, and Gaddafi's demoralized mercenary army rapidly dissolved, many fleeing across the border to Chad, Niger, and Mali. By October, the opposition controlled the entire country. Gaddafi, found hiding in a drain pipe outside of Tripoli, was captured and killed.

Syria: descent into civil war

Like the other personalist Arab regimes, Syria featured a hated, corrupt ruling family, great inequality, and a large frustrated youth bulge. But its ruler, Bashar al-Assad, felt he was secure. He believed his opposition to Israel gave him popularity, unlike the pro-Western regimes in Tunisia and Egypt. Also, Syria was still a tribal, sectarian society. Assad's family came from a small and cohesive Shi'a minority, the Alawites—and Assad had packed the military with loyal Alawite officers.

Nonetheless, emboldened by the other Arab revolutions, and especially the intervention of NATO against Gaddafi in March, young Syrians began a campaign of nonviolent resistance. It began with demonstrations in the small southern town of Deraa. Had Assad shown restraint, perhaps the movement could have been contained. But as in Tunisia, the regime's indiscriminate and brutal response to initial protests, captured on YouTube and spread by overseas Syrians anxious to see regime change, quickly spread across the country on satellite television.

At first, the commercial center of Aleppo and the capital, Damascus, were quiet. Troops were dispatched to the smaller cities where protests had developed to deal with what they were told were traitors and foreign jihadists. But upon finding they had been sent to kill ordinary Syrians, many refused to shoot. Some were executed by their commanders, but this only increased the number of those willing to defect.

By late 2011 the regime changed its strategy. Instead of sending troops on the ground to attack protestors, artillery and planes were used to bomb neighborhoods held by rebels, and then special forces, dominated by loyal Alawites, were sent to clear the area. Though effective, the regime did not have enough troops to carry out such operations in more than a few places at a time. The opposition became adept at melting away in response to such attacks and reconstituting itself in other regions, but it also became clear that peaceful protests would not be effective against Assad. The rebels too changed their strategy, seeking to capture weapons and creating military units led by defecting soldiers to carry out civil war.

Throughout 2012 resistance spread, reaching Aleppo and Damascus. But the regime's core military forces held fast and repelled each assault. The rebels waited for the world to intervene to help overturn the tyrant, as in Libya. They waited in vain. China and Russia blocked any UN resolutions to aid the opposition. The United States and Europe were wary of yet another engagement in the region. The battle on the ground was already too complex for a no-fly zone or targeted strikes on Assad's forces to be decisive; and western countries worried that simply shipping weapons to the opposition would result in even more deaths and that the weapons would find their way into the hands of jihadists. Meanwhile, Iran, determined to protect its supply route to Hezbollah in Lebanon and anxious to support a fellow Shi'a regime, intervened to support Assad, providing money, weapons, and military advisors.

By early 2013 the struggle in Syria had become a major civil war, with tens of thousands killed, sectarian conflicts inflamed, and jihadists moving into local power vacuums. Large parts of Aleppo and Damascus were in ruins, and battles raged throughout the country. While the insurgency was slowly gaining strength, Assad showed no indication that he might depart. Deaths mounted with no immediate end in sight.

The absence of revolutions in the Arab monarchies

Tunisia, Egypt, Libya, and Syria fit a common profile of states that suffer revolutions: A corrupt personalist regime that alienates elites and loses the loyalty of the military, facing popular grievances fueled by fiscal and economic strains and demographic pressures. In all these cases a broad opposition coalition formed around a narrative of injustice featuring greedy ruling families abusing their beleaguered people: "You dress in the latest fashions," crowds in Cairo roared at Mubarak, "while we sleep twelve to a room!" In Tunisia and Egypt, the army refused to defend the regime, and the rulers were quickly pushed aside. In Libya and Syria, portions of the army stiffened by tribal and sectarian loyalty did defend the regime but had limited capacity. In Libya, foreign intervention by NATO allowed the rebels to defeat Gaddafi in a few months. But in Syria foreign intervention was on the side of the Assad regime, allowing it to keep fighting. The causal factors and processes of these revolutions are thus familiar, following the patterns observed in revolutions throughout history.

But what of the Arab countries where no revolution occurred? After all, youth bulges, stagnant wages, and anger at self-serving elites existed from Morocco to Saudi Arabia; why did revolutions occur only in a handful of states?

First, only these four states and Yemen (where protests also drove the ruler, President Saleh, from power) were personalist regimes, whose predations alienated the broader business and military elites, and where opposition anger could focus on one leader and his family and cronies. Most other Arab states are monarchies, such as Morocco, Jordan, Oman, the Gulf Emirates, and Saudi Arabia. In these states, rulers could more easily shift blame to prime ministers and thus retain their position while promising constitutional reforms, which is exactly what happened. Algeria and Iraq, the remaining major Arab states, had recently been tested in civil wars in which they had overcome their opposition. The oil-rich countries also had exceptional resources to defend themselves and used them to provide generous grants and subsidies to their militaries and populations. Finally, withdrawal of international support for the regime, or active intervention against it, occurred only in Tunisia, Egypt, and Libya. In Syria, both Russia and Iran supported the regime; Bahrain's ruler received ample support from Saudi Arabia for harsh repression of popular protests, and in Morocco and Jordan the rulers obtained financial backing from other Arab countries.

The Arab Revolutions of 2011 clearly show that when several states in a region enter an unstable equilibrium, a wave of revolutions can spread quickly through them. Yet viewing the region as a whole, we are reminded that it takes many conditions coming together for a successful revolution to occur. Indeed, across all of North Africa and the Middle East, only four nations—Tunisia, Egypt, Libya, and Yemen—have toppled their rulers as of early 2013. The fact that multiple conditions must come together to create a revolution has kept them rare and special events across history.

Moreover, even where dictators were overthrown, the road ahead has proven rocky. In Tunisia, the most peaceful of the four, the

Islamist party (Ennahda) entered power-sharing agreements with secular parties, and the major political groups cooperated on producing a new constitution. Yet even there cooperation has been shaken by the assassination of popular secular politicians, and the consolidation of democracy is not assured.

In Libya, secular, tribal, and Islamist militias all continue to act independently, defying efforts to create a civilian-controlled national security force. Many towns have been riven by militia violence and political assassinations, including an attack on the U.S. diplomatic mission in Benghazi that killed a U.S. ambassador. New laws banning anyone who served in Libya's government under Gaddafi from holding office in the new regime have led several ministers to resign and raised questions about where experienced officials can be found. It may be many months before Libya has a government that is fully in charge of the country.

In Egypt, events have followed a typical revolutionary trajectory, from honeymoon to polarization, then counter-revolution. Following the joy and outburst of new political parties formed in the wake of Mubarak's departure, politics devolved into a struggle for power between the two best-organized groups remaining in Egyptian society—the army and the Muslim Brotherhood. Secular liberal groups, despite their early leadership role, lacked a grass-roots base of support or national organization, and were increasingly marginalized. When the Brotherhood candidate Mohammed Morsi won Egypt's first-ever free election for President, he signaled that he intended to pack Parliament, the judiciary, and the constitutional drafting committee with Islamists and sought to drive the army out of political life. His actions provoked a popular backlash and retribution by the military. Drawing on growing fears that the Brotherhood intended to impose a fundamentalist Islamic regime, and with considerable popular support, the army deposed Morsi and passed emergency laws to reimpose military rule. Yet the army attack on the Brotherhood led to many hundreds of deaths; the likely outcome is the rise of even more radical Islamist groups and more violence before a stable regime emerges.

Finally, in Yemen, although the former personalist ruler Ali Abdullah Saleh has left office, his successor is struggling to form a stable government and maintain control of the country. Hundreds of new parties have formed, regional secession movements have revived, and radical Islamist groups have sought to set up bases in the provinces (where they are targeted by U.S. drone strikes that further raise opposition to the government). It is difficult to tell whether Yemen is gradually building a new central government or is gradually sliding into chaos.

In sum, it is far too early to tell what the outcome of the Arab Revolutions of 2011 will be. What we can be certain of, in the short run, is that they will unfold as all revolutions do: with ongoing struggles for power between radicals and moderates, a key role for foreign intervention, difficulty in imposing central authority on rebellious localities, and years of uncertainty before settled governments emerge.

Chapter 11
The future of revolutions

When I was still a graduate student in 1979, as the Nicaraguan and Iranian Revolutions were unfolding, I expressed my excitement to colleagues about these events. We felt these were fascinating, but at the same time we wondered if there would be any more revolutions in the years ahead. After all, revolutions had arisen mainly in monarchies and empires, hardly any of which remained. Centralized party-states, like those ruling communist countries, seemed immune to revolution. And dictatorships, like those in Iran and Nicaragua, would likely be more strongly supported by the United States as long as the Cold War continued.

But the years ahead continued to fill with revolutions: the anti-apartheid revolution in South Africa; the Philippines' "People Power" Revolution that overthrew Ferdinand Marcos; the Polish Solidarity Revolution, the Czechoslovak Velvet Revolution, and the other anticommunist revolutions in Eastern Europe and the Soviet Union; the Maoist Revolution in Nepal; the Orange Revolution in the Ukraine; and the Arab Revolutions of 2011, to name only the most prominent.

In the decades since the 1980s, world politics has continued to be shaped by revolutions. The collapse of the Soviet Union was as momentous as the collapse of the Russian, German, and Austro-Hungarian Empires after World War I. The success of multiple "color revolutions" has provided a compelling new model for nonviolent resistance and regime change. And the revolutions that swept across North Africa and the Middle East in 2010–12 have shaken the relationships among the United States, the Arab nations, and Israel that governed the region for decades.

There has been a marked shift in the dominant type of revolution. Nicaragua and Iran were the last revolutions to produce ideologically driven radical regimes. Since then, revolutions have produced weak democracies or pragmatic semiauthoritarian regimes. Recent revolutions have also more often been nonviolent, although the examples of Nepal, where a violent guerrilla movement battled to force a change of government, and of Syria, where thousands have perished in the struggle against the Assad regime, show that violent revolutions can still occur.

What is the likely future of revolutions? They will continue to occur where regimes exhibit the five conditions that lead to state breakdown—an economic or fiscal crisis; elites that are divided and alienated from the regime; a coalition among popular groups with diverse grievances; the emergence of a persuasive narrative of resistance; and an international environment favorable to revolutionary change. These conditions seem most likely to arise in sub-Saharan Africa, which exhibits both rapid population growth and multiple governments that are either personalist regimes or weak, corrupt democracies. Authoritarian leaders in the Middle East, central Asia, and south and southeast Asia will also become vulnerable when their natural resource wealth grows too weak to support their patronage regimes. Even communist China is showing signs of all five conditions emerging, although it remains unclear whether they will arise in a combination that leads to a sudden collapse of the regime, or mount slowly in a manner that will produce a negotiated revolution, with rising popular pressure leading to reforms that transform the government and its role in society.

A further lesson from history is that we should not expect most revolutions to suddenly create stable democracies. Revolutions create new dilemmas and unleash new struggles for power. Most revolutions, including even the American Revolution of 1776, went through more than one constitution, discriminated against minorities, and veered toward weak government or back toward authoritarian tendencies before achieving steady progress toward democracy.

Someday, all countries in the world will have stable, resilient, inclusive, and just regimes. At that point, perhaps revolutions will fade into history with other heroic tales of wars and the creation of states and peoples. But we are a long way from that day. Indeed, in recent years, the number and quality of democracies in the world has been declining. So we will continue to see people mobilizing to overturn their governments in pursuit of social justice and creating new political institutions.

If the trends of the last thirty years continue, they will increasingly do so by nonviolent resistance and avoid the terrors of radical revolutions that prize ideological purity over human life. We can then hope that in the future the heroism of revolutions will predominate, while the horrors will more often be avoided. Yet it will likely take more wisdom, and more cooperation among people of different faiths and races, than we have today to reach that goal.

References

Chapter 1

"No Sire, it is a *revolution*!": *Webster's New World Dictionary of Quotations* (Hoboken, NJ: Chambers Harrap), http://quotes .yourdictionary.com/rochefoucauld.

Chapter 2

"We of the older generations may not live to see the decisive battles": Vladimir I. Lenin, "Lecture on the 1905 Revolution," in *Lenin: Collected Works* (Moscow: Progress Publishers, 1964), 23:253.

Chapter 4

"The King has been taken away by poor men": Alan H. Gardiner, *The Admonitions of an Egyptian Sage from a Hieratic Papyrus in Leiden* (Leipzig: J. C. Hinrichs'sche Buchhandlung, 1909), 16, 35, 53, 58.

"Death thus raged in every shape": Thucydides, *The Peloponnesian War*, [431 BCE], trans. Richard Crawley (New York: Random House, 1982), 198.

Chapter 5

"That the people are, under God, the original of all just power": George Macaulay Trevelyan, *England Under the Stuarts* (London: Routledge, 2002), 276.

From the English Bill of Rights (1689): English Bill of Rights 1689,
"An Act Declaring the Rights and Liberties of the Subject and
Settling the Succession of the Crown," http://avalon.law.yale
.edu/17th_century/england.asp.

Chapter 6

"England hath been known for hundreds of years": Oliver Cromwell,
"At the Opening of Parliament Under the Protectorate," 1654,
http://www.bartleby.com/268/3/11.html.

"Give me Liberty or give me Death!": Patrick Henry, "Give Me
Liberty or Give Me Death," March 23, 1775, speech to the Virginia
House of Burgesses, http://www.nationalcenter.org/GiveMe
Liberty.html.

"deriving their just powers from the consent of the governed":
Thomas Jefferson, "The Declaration of Independence," 1776,
http://www.archives.gov/exhibits/charters/declaration_
transcript.html.

"What Is the Third Estate?": Abbé Emmanuel Joseph Sieyès, "What
Is the Third Estate?", originally published in Paris, France in 1789,
http://faculty.smu.edu/rkemper/cf_3333/Sieyes_What_is_the_
Third_Estate.pdf, 120.

Thomas Paine on the worthlessness of kings: Thomas Paine, *Common
Sense*, Philadelphia, February 14, 1776, "Of Monarchy and
Hereditary Succession," http://www.ushistory.org/paine/
commonsense/sense3.htm.

Thomas Jefferson on natural rights: Thomas Jefferson, "The
Declaration of Independence," 1776, http://www.archives.gov/
exhibits/charters/declaration_transcript.html.

The Meiji Constitution of 1889 on the rights of Japanese subjects:
"The Constitution of the Empire of Japan (1989)," Hanover
Historical Texts Project, http://history.hanover.edu/texts/
1889con.html.

Chapter 7

"history will absolve me": Fidel Castro, "History will Absolve Me,"
speech delivered 1953, Castro Internet Archive, http://www
.marxists.org/history/cuba/archive/castro/1953/10/16.htm.

Chapter 10

"Egypt's foreign minister dismissed the idea": Cited by Marc Lynch, *The Arab Uprising* (New York: Public Affairs: 2012), 81.

"People who don't love me don't deserve to live": ibid., 170.

"while we sleep twelve to a room!": Ann Ciezadlo, "Let them Eat Bread," *Foreign Affairs.com*, March 23, 3011, http://www.foreignaffairs.com/articles/67672/annia-ciezadlo/let-them-eat-bread#.

Further reading

What is a revolution?

Foran, John. *Taking Power: On the Origins of Third World Revolutions*. Cambridge: Cambridge University Press, 2005.

Goldstone, Jack A. *Revolution and Rebellion in the Early Modern World*. Berkeley: University of California Press, 1991.

Goodwin, Jeff. *No Other Way Out: States and Revolutionary Movements, 1945–1991*. Cambridge: Cambridge University Press, 2001.

Katz, Mark N. *Revolutions and Revolutionary Waves*. New York: Palgrave Macmillan, 1999.

Moore, Barrington, Jr. *Origins of Dictatorship and Democracy*. Boston: Beacon Press, 1966.

Nepstad, Sharon E. *Nonviolent Revolutions: Civil Resistance in the Late 20th Century*. New York: Oxford University Press, 2011.

Parsa, Misagh. *States, Ideologies, and Social Revolutions: A Comparative Analysis of Iran, Nicaragua, and the Philippines*. Cambridge: Cambridge University Press, 2000.

Selbin, Eric. *Revolution, Rebellion, and Resistance*. London: Zed Books, 2010.

Skocpol, Theda. *States and Social Revolutions: A Comparative Analysis of France, Russia and China*. Cambridge: Cambridge University Press, 1979.

Specific revolutions

DeFronzo, James. *Revolutionary Movements in World History: From 1750 to the Present.* 3 vols. Santa Barbara, CA: ABC CLIO, 2006.

Goldstone, Jack A., ed., *The Encyclopedia of Political Revolutions.* Washington, DC: CQ Press, 1998.

Revolutions in the ancient world

Forrest, William George. *The Emergence of Greek Democracy.* New York: McGraw-Hill, 1979.

Ober, Josiah. *The Athenian Revolution.* Princeton, NJ: Princeton University Press, 1998.

Shaban, M. A. *The Abbasid Revolution.* Cambridge: Cambridge University Press, 1979.

Syme, Ronald. *The Roman Revolution.* Oxford: Oxford University Press, 2002.

Revolutions of the Renaissance and Reformation

Kishlansky, Mark. *A Monarchy Transformed: Britain 1603–1714.* London: Penguin, 1996.

Pincus, Steven. *1688: The First Modern Revolution.* New Haven, CT: Yale University Press, 2011.

Weinstein, Donald. *Savonarola: The Rise and Fall of a Renaissance Prophet.* New Haven, CT: Yale University Press, 2011.

Worden, Blair. *The English Civil Wars 1640–1660.* London: Orion, 2009.

Constitutional revolutions

Bailyn, Bernard. *The Ideological Origins of the American Revolution.* Cambridge, MA: Harvard University Press, 1992.

Doyle, William. *The Oxford History of the French Revolution.* Oxford: Oxford University Press, 2003.

Huber, Thomas. *The Revolutionary Origins of Modern Japan.* Stanford, CA: Stanford University Press, 1990.

Jansen, Marius B. *The Making of Modern Japan.* Cambridge, MA: Harvard University Press, 2002.

Kaiser, Thomas, and Dale Van Kley, eds. *From Deficit to Deluge: The Origins of the French Revolution.* Stanford, CA: Stanford University Press, 2010.

Klooster, Wim. *Revolutions in the Atlantic World*. New York: New York University Press, 2009.

Sperber, Jonathan. *The European Revolutions, 1848–1851*. Cambridge: Cambridge University Press, 2005.

Wood, Gordon S. *The Creation of the American Republic 1776–1787*. Chapel Hill: University of North Carolina Press, 1998.

Communist revolutions

Fitzpatrick, Sheila. *The Russian Revolution*. 3rd ed. Oxford: Oxford University Press, 2008.

Pérez-Stable, Marifeli. *The Cuban Revolution: Origins, Course and Legacy*. 3rd ed. New York: Oxford University Press, 2012.

Spence, Jonathan. *The Search for Modern China*. 3rd ed. New York: W. W. Norton, 2013.

Trotsky, Leon. *A History of the Russian Revolution*. Translated by Max Eastman. Chicago: Haymarket Books, 2008.

Revolutions against dictators

Booth, John. *The End and the Beginning: The Nicaraguan Revolution*. Boulder, CO: Westview, 1985.

Keddie, Nikki. *Modern Iran: Roots and Results of Revolution*. New Haven, CT: Yale University Press, 2006.

Kurzman, Charles. *The Unthinkable Revolution in Iran*. Cambridge, MA: Harvard University Press, 2005.

Womack, John. *Zapata and the Mexican Revolution*. New York: Vintage Books, 1968.

Color revolutions

Ash, Timothy Garton. *The Magic Lantern: The Revolution of '89 Witnessed in Warsaw, Budapest, Berlin, and Prague*. New York: Vintage, 1993.

Aslund, Anders, and Michael McFaul, eds. *Revolution in Orange: The Origins of Ukraine's Democratic Breakthrough*. Washington, DC: Carnegie Endowment for International Peace, 2006.

Beissinger, Mark. *Nationalist Mobilization and the Collapse of the Soviet State*. Cambridge: Cambridge University Press, 2002.

Bunce, Valerie J., and Sharon L. Wolchik. *Defeating Authoritarian Leaders in Postcommunist Countries*. Cambridge: Cambridge University Press, 2011.

Kotkin, Stephen. *Armageddon Averted: The Soviet Collapse 1970–2000*. New York: Oxford University Press, 2008.

Thompson, Mark R. *The Anti-Marcos Struggle: Personalistic Rule and Democratic Transition in the Philippines*. New Haven, CT: Yale University Press, 2011.

The Arab revolutions of 2011

Cook, Steven A. *The Struggle for Egypt: From Nasser to Tahrir Square*. New York: Oxford University Press, 2011.

Lynch, Marc. *The Arab Uprising: The Unfinished Revolutions of the New Middle East*. New York: Public Affairs, 2012.

Index

Index